IRON
CURTAIN
RISING

IRON CURTAIN RISING

BY PETER LAUFER

A personal journey through the changing landscape of Eastern Europe

FOREWORD BY RAINER HILDEBRANDT

Mercury House, Incorporated
San Francisco

Published in the United States by
Mercury House
San Francisco, California

Mercury House and colophon are registered trademarks
of Mercury House, Incorporated

Printed on recycled, acid-free paper
Manufactured in the United States of America

Library of Congress Cataloging-in-Publication Data

Laufer, Peter.
  Iron curtain rising ; a personal journey through the changing landscape of Eastern Europe / by Peter Laufer.
    p. cm.
    ISBN 1-56279-015-3
    1. Europe, Eastern — Description and travel. 2. Europe, Eastern — History — 1989-. 3. Laufer, Peter — Journeys — Europe, Eastern. I. Title.
DJK18.L38   1991
914.704 — dc20   91-11997
                                                     CIP

with love to

Sheila

for the inspiration

CONTENTS

PREFACE

"Prague? Where's that?"
—AT&T long distance operator, January 1991

I've spent just about as much time during the last three years in dreary, gray Eastern Europe as I've spent at home in sunny California. I'm not complaining. Rubbing shoulders with revolutionaries dumping their oppressors is thrilling. But I've been reminded a few times that things and places now second nature to me might still remain foreign to many readers. Most Westerners are intrigued with the changes in Eastern Europe, but not to the point of immersing themselves there. A colleague of mine made that clear when we were talking about Germany. He's quite well informed; he's a news reporter for an all-news radio station in San Francisco. But he was confused about just where Berlin is located, convinced that it straddled the border separating East and West Germany.

We all specialize in something. He's much more current on California politics than most people.

Driving across the Magyar plains, my friend Markos Kounalakis and I were figuring out our route from Budapest to Sofia. Markos is another journalist from San Francisco. We crossed paths in Germany before the Wall came down and ended up traveling together through much of the excitement of 1989 and 1990. As we were heading for Sofia, he was considering a teaching job in Ohio. He studied the road map labeled Mitteleuropa, checking highways and places by now so familiar to us. Suddenly he looked up at me and said, "I'd better take this job in Ohio. I'm getting to know Europe better than America. I know how to get to Sofia, but I don't know my way from Cleveland to Columbus."

So this preface is designed for those readers who know the interstates better than the autobahns. It's a quick rundown of what's where. Like the program at a ball game, it should make it easier to figure out who the players are, what they're doing to each other, and why.

The Iron Curtain separated Eastern and Western Europe for over forty years. It ran south from the Baltic, splitting the territory that constituted prewar Germany into East Germany and West Germany. It continued on south to cut between West Germany and Czechoslovakia and ran on to divide Austria and its old empire partner, Hungary. The Iron Curtain finally ended on the Adriatic between Italy and Yugoslavia. The Berlin Wall, though a part of the Iron Curtain, was removed geographically from the line that cut through Europe creating Eastern and Western Europe. The Wall circled the western half of Berlin, preventing East Germans from entering the part of Berlin that became a Western enclave when the four winning Allies decided which of them would administer what sections of conquered Germany. Berlin fell into the Soviet sector of Germany, but the capital city was itself divided among the four. So West Berlin became a political island in the heart of East Germany.

Winston Churchill named and defined the Iron Curtain in 1946. "From Stettin in the Baltic to Trieste in the Adriatic," he told an audience at Fulton, Missouri, "an iron curtain has descended across the Continent." Until the mid 1980s, this Iron Curtain made travel and trade between Eastern and Western Europe laborious and, at some times for some people, impossible. The border became more porous as the cold war waned. In the year before the Berlin Wall fell and the Iron Curtain rose, the borders were being described as Swiss cheese because of all the holes.

Some of the holes in the Iron Curtain were literally holes, like those on the border between Italy and Yugoslavia. There, by the late 1980s, travel between the two countries differed very little from that between countries on any normal international border. Although the paperwork required was extreme for travel between Austria and Hungary, that border, too, opened in the eighties.

Other holes, like those made in the Wall separating Berlin, were much more difficult to make. But even the East German regime was allowing more and more travel opportunities to its corralled citizens before the Wall opened.

Most observers, from Western diplomats to those of us wandering back and forth from East to West just because we were curious, assumed the Wall and the Iron Curtain would not suddenly disappear but would simply become irrelevant. We figured the restrictions on movement between Eastern and Western Europe would disappear first, and then the physical barriers would fade away, unneeded.

No one forecast the suddenness of the changes late in 1989 that opened the Berlin Wall and removed the physical Iron Curtain from the frontiers of East Germany and Czechoslovakia.

As late as January 1989, less than a year before the Wall crumbled, Erich Honecker was still running East Germany. His picture looked out from walls all over the country, usually from a deep blue background. The result was not the heavenly touch his handlers intended. Instead, the softness of the blue accentuated his harsh features, drawing attention to the cruelty of his rule. The Wall will still be in place in fifty and even a hundred years, Honecker insisted, to protect East Germany from those who want to "disturb stability and peace in Europe."[1]

But it wasn't just Honecker. American diplomats in Berlin were reacting to President Reagan's call for the Wall to be torn down with the Swiss cheese response. Off the record, they called

---

[1]Honecker made his faulty projections at a speech to the organizers of a celebration commemorating the five hundredth anniversary of peasant revolt hero Thomas Münzer. At about the same time, the East German newspaper *Junge Welt* responded to the right-wing Republikaner Party election victories in West Germany with a reiteration of the official rationalization for the Berlin Wall: "The significance of the term 'anti-fascist protection Wall,'" *Junge Welt* explained to its readers, "therefore is not antiquated and outdated, as claimed repeatedly by some in the West."

Reagan's speech just politics and predicted as a more likely scenario a slow improvement of conditions along the borders.

Now, the Iron Curtain is gone, with only misfit Albania holding out in Europe and bucking the revolutions of 1989. There travel in and out is still severely restricted, almost negligible. But even in Albania, protest and reform began by 1990. And throughout the rest of Eastern Europe, the Iron Curtain is becoming a memory, as we all struggle to sort out the post–cold-war Europe.

A few words are in order about the terminology I've decided to use. Dictatorships were imposed by the Soviet Union on the Eastern European countries it conquered during World War II. Those governments called themselves Communists and Socialists and a variety of other names that turned out to be just euphemisms for dictatorships. The Americans called them all Communists, which became a catchword for a feared enemy. For convenience, especially because we've become so used to hearing the term, I've chosen to refer to the old Eastern bloc governments collectively as Communists, with an uppercase C. It turns out to be less confusing than trying to keep track of the names the governing dictators made up for themselves, like Socialist Unity Party in East Germany or Hungarian Socialists' Workers Party. But it's important to remember that the Communists in power after the war in Eastern Europe set up systems that were nothing like the utopian ideal of communism.

Eastern Europe stinks. Make no mistake about it. It is Eastern Europe, and it does stink. The air is so thick from pollution that you can taste it. The stench of the strong cigarettes, the brown coal, the awful-smelling government soap, and all the other smells combine to create an overall aroma that is different in the East. Attitudes too, after a couple of generations of oppression, are different.

Once the Iron Curtain parted, attempts were made by some frustrated boosters of Poland, Czechoslovakia, Hungary, and Yugoslavia to get the world to refer to them as Middle Europe, not Eastern Europe. They used to be called Middle Europe, before they were cordoned off behind the Iron Curtain. Maybe,

someday in the future, they will be called Middle Europe again.
But it is toying with reality to suddenly stop calling the Europe
lying east of the rising Iron Curtain, Eastern Europe. Despite
the revolutions of 1989, the elections of 1990, and the continuing positive changes in the old Soviet satellites, the differences
foisted on Eastern Europe since World War II will take at least a
generation to erase.

The good news for those of us who are attached to that part of
the world is that positive change is occurring there faster than
we imagined—just a couple of years ago—such change would
be possible.

Peter Laufer
Sausalito, California
January 1991

FOREWORD

I am writing these words in the Checkpoint Charlie Museum office. Very recently, a representative of the U.S. military headquarters brought us the legendary sign that says in four languages: You Are Leaving the American Sector. Soon after the successful and peaceful revolution, some souvenir hunters tried to steal it and had already sawed through its post. A passerby, just in time, was able to interfere and called the police. The sign will help people in the future realize the meaning of a place where world history revealed itself. Here the victorious World War II powers and both Germanys faced each other. An alert observer of thieves has helped preserve a piece of tangible history.

Throughout history, the witnesses of revolutionary times and events rarely remain in the role of contemplative observers. What they are watching and what is attracting them is much too important to them, and so must not get lost.

Peter Laufer seismographically recorded the political earthquake at many scenes. He spoke with apparatchiks and their victims, with those who were misled and those who thought ahead, with people in conflict and with bystanders. He watched them, and he was curious and inquisitive enough to get into some trouble himself.

The earthquake only brings to the surface what, over the years, has been taking place deep inside the earth. But we are only people made of flesh and blood; we are all people just like you and me. The first seconds of an earthquake's effect are most significant. And we are still feeling this political earthquake; we do not yet know the course of events in the Soviet Union, in Romania, Bulgaria, Albania.

It was believed all over the world that the East-West confrontation was a cemented balance that allowed the two German states to come together only gradually, and only under the umbrella of an all-European approach. Things happened differently; the radiation of *glasnost* and the power of the opposition's peaceful struggle in the Eastern European countries had been underestimated.

Not by Peter Laufer. And that is why his work is not only an exciting and close-up report, but also provides those flash pictures that will permit coming generations to understand the perspectives and connections of what happened.

Rainer Hildebrandt
Berlin
1991

After working during his student days as a Nazi resister, and then after World War II against the Communists, Dr. Rainer Hildebrandt founded the Checkpoint Charlie Museum. The museum documents the construction of the Berlin Wall, displays art inspired by the Wall, and is filled with the actual contraptions refugees used over the years to escape over, under, and through the Iron Curtain.

Chapter One

THEY CAN'T KILL ALL OF US

"Hurry, McDonald's is still open!"
— One East German yelling to another as they race
through the opening Berlin Wall, November 9, 1989

FOR ANNETTE GOLDBERG'S husband, the Iron Curtain stood as an obstacle for another week or two after the East German government opened the Berlin Wall and dropped travel restrictions for its citizens. I picked him up on the road to Dresden; he was hitchhiking and talked fast and nonstop about the changes. He looked like a late-sixties Berkeley student: long hair, ragged cloth overcoat, John Lennon glasses. On his way to pick up a fixed bicycle, he graciously and voraciously accepted some West German chocolate. He wanted to visit the West, especially Berlin, but he hadn't yet applied for the needed exit visa. That's because Annette had thrown his pants in the wash just as the Wall opened. She washed his pants with his identity card still in a pocket, ruining it. He couldn't apply for the still-needed visa without his *Ausweiss*.

But after years of government oppression, he was happy. A poorly timed washing mistake wasn't going to dampen his enthusiasm and excitement. He was comfortable and confident that there was no need to rush West. Along with the rest of Eastern Europe, he was convinced that now the Iron Curtain had parted, it wasn't going to close on him again.

The Iron Curtain rising in the autumn of 1989 marked the most exciting period of European history since the black days of

1

Nazi atrocities and the miseries of World War II. Although the victory of the Allies was, of course, good news, the postwar period continued to be difficult and frustrating for much of Europe; the mood was sad and oppressive as the conflict turned into the cold war between the West and the Soviets.

But the revolutionary successes that roared through the Eastern bloc in 1989 were not just exciting examples of people taking power. They were joyous celebrations of the human spirit at its best. Millions of people saw their historical moment of opportunity, grabbed it, and freed themselves.

What followed in the next few months, during the free-for-all between the overthrow of the Communist dictators and the first free elections in a couple of generations, was simply unbelievable for those of us lucky enough to be there watching and participating.

Since 1980, I've made several trips through Eastern Europe. In 1988, I moved to Berlin for a year. A few months after I returned to California in 1989, the Wall opened, and I rushed back to participate, staying on in Europe for the revolution a week later in Czechoslovakia. I returned to Eastern Europe again for the 1990 elections and the unification of Germany. I lived through the remarkable transitions, seeing the landscape change. I watched as the enemy most American baby boomers grew up to fear and hate turned into just another bargain tourist attraction. I met the people forcing the Iron Curtain to rise, and saw authoritarian repression junked and replaced with renewed human hope.

It seemed to start so quickly, so unexpectedly. Suddenly the incredible images were everywhere, epitomized by the all-night celebration party on the Wall. Just months before that wild night I was living in an old Berlin tenement, a few blocks from the line between Us and Them. I crossed often. It was never routine.

The drab and stark border architecture itself became somewhat familiar, though never boring. The structures always caught my attention: poorly maintained fake wood, crumbling concrete, the gray booth the guard sat in, chair positioned high—that way he always looked down on you as he checked your passport.

Paranoia and suspicion were always the guard's message. Without smiling he (and it invariably was a he) took your papers and checked your face against your picture. Then he double-checked, often triple-checked, as if for some unfathomable reason you might be trying to sneak into East Germany.

Once you passed that test, the windowless door to the East buzzed long enough for you to push it open. It was a loud, irritating, authoritarian buzz. So was the slam of the door as it sprang back into the locked position after you passed through.

I didn't always pass through without trouble. I was arrested and searched, lost property and time when my attitude was not correct or my papers weren't in order.

Suddenly that barrier was gone, replaced with smiling, helpful guards. The buzzing door was held open by the surging crowd of border-crossers. And the guards didn't bark nasty commands to shut it.

Just months before those wild celebrations, the last miserable East German was killed trying to escape, and a friend of mine in West Germany was fighting the East German authorities merely to get permission to cross back into the other side to join her mother's seventieth birthday party.

★   ★   ★

Only months before the barrier opened, an East German bus driver talked about his confinement and his dreams while making the trip from East Berlin to Potsdam. The route was round-about; the detour was required to avoid driving through West Berlin.

We looked out at the snaking length of Wall running parallel to the road. From the East side, without its colorful graffiti, the Wall sometimes looked less intimidating, just another slab of concrete in the dismal cityscape. The viewing platforms and political statements covering the West side drew more attention to the restriction the Wall sliced through Berlin than the bare concrete on the East side.

"I watch 'Miami Vice,'" the bus driver told me, "and I see the beach and women and life." Then he gestured out the window at the gray drizzle and Stalinist architecture. "And here I am," he muttered.

"There are advantages and disadvantages to everything," the driver said in a resigned voice. He tried to accept the Party line, making a halfhearted case for the advantages the Wall provided East Germany as a blockade against terrorism and crime.

Then he pointed to the Wall. "This is the biggest problem, that we cannot travel."

The theme was repeated as we made our way toward Potsdam.

"Life is good. We have what we want, and it is cheap—except for travel," he said. And a few other things. "I've been waiting ten years for a telephone, and I still do not have one."

He talked cars. He pointed out the cheapest, the little Trabant that costs a ten-year wait, not to mention full payment in cash. And a used car is "much more expensive," he smiled, "because there is no wait."

He drove on through the gray.

"It is the dream of all drivers to drive a truck across America, just one time." He grabbed an imaginary cord and blasted an imaginary trucker's air horn, all the while insisting that he probably would come home to East Germany if given the chance to travel. He would come home to his family, hometown, and job.

As a trained worker, his opportunities for travel were limited. He was reminded repeatedly by his government whenever he contemplated a vacation that a trip outside the Eastern bloc was not allowed for him. He was too valuable as a worker; the government didn't want to risk losing him to the lures of the West.

Just months before the Wall opened, the East German government mocked changes in the Soviet Union; it censored *Pravda*, and then promised that the Berlin Wall would be a required fixture for generations.

"Would you," insisted one old East German politburo member, "when your neighbor puts up new wallpaper, also feel obliged to repaper your home?"[1]

But the old-line leadership didn't expect the Hungarians to allow East Germans like the bus driver to cross the Iron Curtain through that fellow Warsaw Pact country. The old East German Communists didn't expect their own protégés — the East German border guards — to question and violate standing orders to shoot fleeing frustrated fellow East Germans.

So, as the exodus speeded up through the Hungarian rip in the Iron Curtain, the East German economy was gutted of workers. The streetcars sat idle in Leipzig, the motormen escaping to the West. Bakeries were shuttered and empty. It was the same story all around the country. Hospitals were without nurses and doctors; they were seeking their fortunes across the border. Shops closed, the shopkeepers off to the West.

Then, with the Hungarian highways jammed full of escapees, hundreds of thousands of other East Germans braved the threat of arrest or worse, and made their way into the streets of most East German cities, demanding change with the announcement that made the regime realize the Party was over. "*Wir bleiben*," they screamed. "We're staying." The majority decided staying home and fixing the damage was a better option than running away or being chased from their homeland. Shortly they were to decide at the ballot box that being annexed by West Germany was their fastest bet toward a better life, even if it meant losing their separate national identity.

Previously, the East German authorities could easily rid themselves of dissidents; they simply sent them West. Often exiling its citizens was a money-making device for the relatively poor East German government. It sold their freedom in direct return for cash payments from the West German government. The price was usually based on the perceived value of the immigrant. Generally, the better the education, the higher the cost. But now the crowds were refusing the offer of a ticket West. The

---

[1] The oldtimer — Kurt Hager — made his comments to a reporter from *Stern* magazine who had asked him if *perestroika* would ever come to East Germany.

dramatic change in tactics by the frustrated East German people changed the rules of the game permanently.

In a last-ditch attempt to save its power position, the government opened the Wall.

Hours later I was on a Lufthansa jet heading through the night back from California toward the rising Iron Curtain.

I joined the throng smashing the Wall with hammers and chisels. I wandered the streets of East Berlin; the sternness I remembered from just months before had been replaced with laughing, animated, and smiling faces. I watched the crowds pour through the Wall and parade up and down the Kurfürstendamm, buying McDonald's hamburgers and window-shopping in disbelief.

I checked in with friends. A spy novel writer was on the street for days without sleep, taking notes for his next book. "Czechoslovakia before Christmas," he guaranteed me.

★ ★ ★

But the Czechoslovakians didn't wait that long. In less than a week I was jammed in with the masses filling Wenceslas Square in Prague, and by the end of that week the Evil Empire had lost another colony.

The speed of the change was much more of a shock to observers back in America than it was to participants at the scene. From the White House to the man on the street, Americans were numbed by the immediate geopolitical reversal. Not so in Eastern Europe where, with a thankful nod toward Gorbachev, time after time I heard the same refrains: "We've got nothing to lose," or "They can't kill all of us," or "I've got to do this for my children."

I'd been drawn to the Iron Curtain for years: fascinated by its arbitrary construction, disgusted by the misery imposed on the people left on the wrong side of it, but at the same time intrigued by some odd form of romance that their isolation and deprivation offered those of us lucky enough to be able to cross the line, back and forth, whenever we wished.

News reporting work, vacations, and family visits brought me to the border and then in and out of the Communist world where East Germany, Czechoslovakia, Hungary, and Yugoslavia meet the West.

All these connections lured me back to the line of the Iron Curtain. I decided to make the trip along the frontier between East and West before it became a memory. I jumped at the chance to experience the excitement of this revolutionary period, checking back in with my old friends, relatives, and contacts in my old haunts.

★   ★   ★

I wanted to experience scenes like the second-rate hotel where I found myself staying in Prague. In three days, the Stalinist government would be overthrown and a million Czechs and Slovaks would be cheering in the streets.

But the night I got there, paranoia still ran high. Bus-loads of special Communist soldiers were racing into Prague from all over the country, ready to fight the growing street demonstrations. Memories of the tanks that destroyed the Prague Spring remained strong.

A disco ball whirled in the bar, casting reflections off its mirrors. Two Russian businessmen flirted with a tired-looking hooker. At an old turntable, the barmaid's boyfriend played disc jockey. He spun a Czech-language remake of "I Left My Heart in San Francisco" for the two Americans sipping beers.

Slowly the barmaid began to talk, glancing about for her boss and going silent whenever he appeared. Yes, she was out on the streets demonstrating, she said with a strong accent, "I have a six-year-old daughter. I had to be there for her."

★   ★   ★

I looked forward to returning deep into East Germany, to watch remarkable instant changes after years of stagnation, changes like the official recognition of foul air. *Smog* is simply not a strong enough word to conjure up the image of the air in Leipzig. When the winter fog settles in, the factories are cranked up, and the brown coal furnaces are heating the apartment blocks; when the Trabbies spew out their two-cycle engine exhaust and it mixes with the soot from diesel trucks, you cannot see across Marx-Engels-Platz. After a few hours outside, your throat starts to burn. Hotels, because their front doors keep opening, actually fill with the smoke, too. Haze hovers lazily in the lobbies, and porters apologize for the irritating grit that settles over everything.

Yet it was not until late in November 1989 that the local newspaper mentioned smog. The day the air pollution levels were published in the paper was a day of victory for the infant environmental movement. Until that news account, the official government response to complaints was that there was no smog in Leipzig.

"It was a secret before," a Leipzig revolutionary told me as she marveled over the carbon dioxide numbers in the newspaper. "We heard about the smog over West German radio and TV, but it stopped at the Wall, according to the government."

★   ★   ★

I was drawn to experiences that occur only during periods of revolutionary change—layovers like the hour or so I spent on a back road between Dresden and Prague, watching stern Czech border guards scan carefully my stack of suspicious-looking newspapers. The East German papers were particularly interesting for the guards. They could read German; their English was marginal. In November 1989, the newly liberated East German papers expressed solidarity with Czech students protesting government suppression in Prague. The papers were confiscated. East German newspapers confiscated by Czechs as subversive— an idea as bizarre as the decision a year earlier by the crumbling East German regime to forbid Soviet magazines because they were counterrevolutionary. Just days later, the Communist government that employed those Czech guards was thrown out of business.

★   ★   ★

Quickly, I realized that I was also going to watch old prejudices resurface and nationalism rise. A week after the East Germans lifted all travel restrictions out of that country, West Berlin authorities beefed up their watch on who they let into that island city.

Suddenly there was a new inspection lane on the highway heading into West Berlin requiring all cars with East bloc license plates, except cars from East Germany, to stop for a special inspection.

Polish cars were particularly suspect to the West Berlin authorities. I stood watch with a customs inspector as he performed his new job of stopping cars with the distinctive white-on-black license plates and PL national identity tags.

First the agent asks for proof of insurance and a driver's license. The driver of an older, off-white Russian-built Lada produces the documents and is politely asked to get out of the car.

"Do you speak German?" asks the guard.

The answer from the driver is no, and the guard uses hand signals to order all the luggage out of the Lada. He quickly pokes through some personal stuff and then zeros in on a satchel, pointing to a carton of cigarettes.

"This is to sell," charges the guard, as he pulls the cigarettes out of the bag, "and this." The guard points to new clothing, still in its factory wrappings, a new pair of shoes with a smaller pair jammed inside, and children's clothing. "Why are there no children in the car?" he asks.

All four Polish men are out of the car now, gathered around the luggage, not looking too concerned. "This is for my brother," explains the Lada driver, now speaking German without any difficulty. The game is over; the four know that they are caught and will not get into West Berlin this time, at this border crossing. The guard explains the West Berlin law that forbids commercial trading without a license, a law the Poles, by their bored look, clearly know well.

"It's not so much," the driver gives a last try, pointing to the meager pile of poor-quality goods. The official is unmoved; the Lada is turned back toward Poland.

Many of the Ladas, the tiny Polish-built Fiats, and the old West German cars with Polish plates do make it through the checkpoint and then head directly for the giant flea market staged every weekend on a vacant tract of land near Checkpoint Charlie. There, desperate Poles spread out for sale an odd variety

of shoddy goods. Hammers and handsaws, toothpaste and mat-
tresses compete with plastic combs and Ping-Pong paddles.
Michael Jackson iron-on T-shirt stickers and an occasional
wooden Russian doll are exchanged for the valuable and available deutsche marks.

The two-hour drive from Poland to Berlin, a couple of days
outside in the freezing flea market air, and the gamble of being
turned back at the border are worthwhile. If the merchant can
pull in just twenty West marks, the weekend take equals an
average Pole's wage for a month.

The West German customs agent who turned back the Lada
is convinced that it's important to stop the small-time smugglers. "These people are ruining the Polish economy," he says,
by exporting consumer goods scarce back home.

I watched as those West Germany authorities practiced a
double standard at the border. They let East German cars pass
freely without inspection, while they stopped and searched the
Poles and other East bloc travelers. The rationalization was that
East Germans were just coming for a visit, carrying nothing to
sell. That faulty logic was contradicted by the sight of little East
German Trabbies jammed with salable stuff from food to
clothing, one even pulling a trailer with a piano crammed into
it. And signs were up all over the West offering to buy antiques
and other possessions from financially strapped East Germans
for hard Western currency. Buying in West Money, announced
one sign, Toys, Teddies, Dolls, Antique Jewelry and Much More.
The sign was decorated with a photocopy of a hundred-mark
bill. In reality, the West Germans were giving their East German
cousins a break that they denied other Eastern Europeans. The
East Germans had fat bank accounts but full of East marks,
relatively worthless on the world economy, and took advantage
of these opportunities to sell—at bargain basement prices—
whatever their rich West Germany cousins wanted to buy.

East German authorities were aware of the double standard.
They spot-checked cars crossing into the West. In one they
found eight pounds of raisins, twenty tablecloths, thirty pairs of
shoes, fifty salamis, and four antique books. All except the books

were government subsidized goods, heading West for a fast
profit. But most shipments made it through, and the transport-
ers made money. Deprived workers on the East side continued
to smuggle, speculate, and look for new methods of taking
advantage of the suddenly porous borders.

After being turned around at the border with his shabby
collection of black market clothing, the driver of the off-white
Lada summed up his frustration and the purpose of his trip
easily: "This is worth a lot of money in Poland."

His trip probably was profitable later the same day. The odds
are good he found another border crossing and made it through
to the flea market.

★   ★   ★

For me, it was another scene from the show I had come back to
watch—the scrambling for position as first the rules were completely discarded and then a new order established.

Levis, McDonald's, *Playboy*, and really nasty pornography
appear in Hungary. Bulgarian Communists try frantically to
reform before being forced out of business, too. Crowds in
Timişoara threaten the temporary government that took over
after the violent revolution there; other Romanian crowds attack
ethnic Hungarians with clubs. Poles struggle with the sudden
shift to a free market economy that hikes prices of long-cheap
staples almost out of reach. Yugoslavs face civil war. And
Albania holds out: a Stalinist throwback, surrounded by a trans-
formed Eastern Europe convulsed in change.

The fall of 1989 and the spring of 1990 marked a change in all
the known world. It wasn't just Europe that changed. The rising
Iron Curtain knocked out the argument of a Communist threat
to America. It offered the world a real chance to stop preparing
for war and exchange that role for a search for peace.

And during all that excitement, life went on and even got
worse for too many Europeans. For others, the upheaval was a
second chance.

"I have the feeling that time is fixed here, and the revolution
was only on TV," my friend Dagmar wrote from the East side

after she finally managed to convince the visa-issuing authorities to let her go to her mother's birthday celebration.

The comment of another German friend foreshadowed some of the problems that followed the initial euphoria. "The atmosphere," she said of Berlin, "is friendly and relaxed. Just as soon as discussions become political, the spirit is less comfortable."

A cousin wrote from Hungary that the time was ripe to try to reclaim a family farm in Czechoslovakia taken by the Nazis and still held by the Communists.

A journalist colleague told stories of trying to travel into Albania.

The stage was set for adventure; the actors were making history. I was lucky to be there, watching.

Chapter Two

SHOOT TO KILL, ALONG THE GERMAN-GERMAN BORDER

"Mr. Gorbachev, tear down this wall!"
— President Ronald Reagan speaking in Berlin, 1987

"No one thinks the Wall is coming down; no one expects the physical wall to come down in our lifetimes."
— American diplomat in the Berlin mission speculating about the future of Germany, 1988

"It was the most cheerful and peaceful invasion: The East Germans stormed West Germany."
— *Bild* newspaper the Monday after the Wall opened, 1989

"I want my Wall back, only this time make it a little higher."
— Legend on a T-shirt for sale in West Berlin, 1990

AT A WEST BERLIN yuppie birthday party I first heard West German appreciation for the division of Germany. It was June 1988, well over a year before the Wall came down. We were in the Grunewald at a swank restaurant, drinking nice white wine, eating tasty, trendy food. A young woman medical student told me she didn't want to face the challenge from the people she was convinced would come across from the East and compete with her for jobs if the Wall opened. "They're better trained and more ambitious," she whined.

Of course, the Wall no longer protects West Germans from East Germans. Most West Germans were obsessed, in the months following the collapse of the Communists in East Germany, with seducing the East Germans into joining West Germany. It was an unfortunate rush together. Now the world and the Germans are stuck with one Germany. Two different political entities filled with Germans could have been much easier for the world to swallow and would have diffused the exaggerated sense of nationalism and ethnic separation that Germany and most of Eastern Europe suffer from.

★ ★ ★

The year before the Iron Curtain rose, I spent months commuting from West Germany across East Germany to Berlin, and the trip almost became routine for me. Yet crossing East Germany was still confounding, arriving in Berlin still weird.

The simple oddness of being stuck in isolated territory, surrounded by a wall, was always on my mind. There was a definite frontier aspect to life in Berlin then. In some ways, it was similar to the Old West in America. It was an outpost. Food and just about everything else was brought in, the same way the railroads hauled supplies across the American plains. The city was surrounded by hostile forces: threatening Communists instead of Indians. It was an outpost for the West, like the Old West forts. Reagan thanked "all the courageous people living in Berlin" on the twenty-seventh, and last, anniversary of the Wall. Berlin was full of misfits who came to enjoy special privileges allowed there. The idea was to encourage people to come to and stay in the city, despite the Wall. Germans in Berlin could dodge the draft, enjoyed tax breaks, and could live alternative life-styles that were frowned upon in West Germany, the same way the fortune seekers of the Old West found themselves free of the constraints of mainstream American society.

★ ★ ★

The drizzle ends as train number 247, the Cologne-Hannover-Berlin-Warsaw run, makes its way East on an autumn afternoon in 1988. The sun is out briefly. Then, it's raining again, gray. The train pulls out of a storybook station, and some old folks actually wave good-bye with handkerchiefs.

Next we're stopping in the Hannover Hauptbahnhof. I'm in a compartment with six sitting places, about to sit up through the night. There's an older woman sharing the little room. She sees a mouse under the heater.

"That mouse is riding through the Iron Curtain without proper papers," I offer as an attempted joke.

She smiles.

Soon we're sliding across the border into East Germany, past the barbed wire fence and the guard towers. The train plugs along, forced to go slowly, not just because of the bad tracks, but for security reasons, or as they say so poignantly in German: *Kontrolle.*

We stop at Marienborn, just inside East Germany. The train comes to a stop and takes on the border guards at a special siding surrounded by impenetrable walls on both sides and fences topped with barbed wire, all under a watchtower and searchlights. No East German gets on this train for the ride to West Berlin. This is just the transit train, crossing East German territory on the rail corridor carved out as part of the agreement to service Berlin with transportation.

It's gray again, fitting this prison-country. The sky is gray, and the uniforms are gray, and the fences are gray.

The Intershop on the platform is closed. Except for a few foreigners and old people, the station is deserted. Of course it's full of guards, but they blend in with the fencing and wire. They don't seem part of the people on the platform.

And it's quiet.

Such a change from the bustle of the stations at Hannover, Braunschweig, Helmstedt, and other cities in West Germany.

The conductor's whistle blows with the shrill squeak made familiar by World War II movies, and we move on into East Germany, knowing we can get out. From the window I watch East Germans at crossings, waiting in their funny little cars. I see them plowing fields or just watching as the train passes. Most can't get out.

The little stations look bleak, worn, empty. But also, in a disconcerting way, they look refreshingly quiet. They're void of trashy billboards, sloppy, loud snack bars. I feel the familiar calm that comes from the lack of perpetual external stimulants and marks the east side of the Iron Curtain. The drab scene acts on me like a relaxant. It seems to force slowing down — contemplation — much the way the barren Nevada desert does. "What do they do here?" ask the speeding travelers who see Nevada as an obstacle to cross on the way to California. Those of us who have lived in that desert know its rewards. East Germans, too, often talk about the rewards of their oppressed society: tighter family units, friends working together in the face of government adversity.

Eventually the passport officer comes. He's with a partner — not because it's a two-man job, but because one guard must keep an eye on the other. The one who issues the paperwork wears a table around his neck like a cigarette girl. Instead of smokes, he carries the transit visas. Young, polite, with even a trace of a smile, he routinely stamps a visa and manages a friendly *"Auf wiedersehen!"* Nobody forecast the end of the Wall. But in its last year there were indications of change. The border guards opened up slightly, suggesting some humanity, and border procedures became smoother and quicker.

The train plods along past deserted-looking towns. The half dozen or so cars waiting to cross the tracks look like a traffic jam against the backdrop of empty streets. Friends visiting from California, disappointed that they could find no dramatic leftover war damage in Berlin, would find it in these forgotten places. War ruins are sprinkled through these towns and the surrounding countryside.

Finally we're in the last East German station, with plenty of anticrime lights keeping the Wall lit up as we drop off the East German border guards and pass into West Berlin, an island in the heart of East Germany.

★   ★   ★

Another day that year before the Wall crumbled, I'm on my way to East Berlin for the afternoon. First I empty my pockets of Eurochecks, guilders, Greek money, press identification: all the stuff that looks as if it might slow down the crossing. The less that's available for the guards to look at, the faster the inspection.

I walk from my Moabit flat to the U-Bahn, ride it to the Zoo Station, transfer to the S-Bahn, and take the elevated train East. The old wooden cars are jammed, mostly with pensioners. The East German government allows its citizens to travel West after retirement age. It's the productive worker who's forced to stay home or leave close relatives at home as hostages. In fact, if the old folks stay West, it's a blessing; then the government saves paying pension money.

We slowly cross over the Wall, looking down on the wide swath of no-man's-land, a cleared space in the middle of Berlin. We pass a watchtower and pull into Friedrichstrasse station.

It, too, is jammed. I find my way through the crowd to the line for foreigners seeking one-day visas. This old train station is doing double duty; the East German government is using it as an international border crossing. There are special lines for West Germans, still another line for West Berliners.

The mood is festive in the foreigners' line, almost like waiting to get into Disneyland. East Berlin is like Commie-land for many travelers, an opportunity to catch a safe glimpse behind the Iron Curtain and get back to the West the same day. The frivolous attitude of the day tourists contrasts abruptly with the grim authoritarian looks of the border guards and their hutches. The trademark East German border guard stare greets each new face: first to the passport picture, then up at the traveler — lingering as if looking for a disguise — and then back to the I.D. for the double check.

The buzzer sounds, unlocking the metal door into East Berlin, spilling me out into the decaying station lobby and the decaying eastern half of the city.

That day business takes me to the American embassy in East Berlin. I look not unlike the East German men walking around: Korean tennis shoes, jeans, ragged sweater, scruffy beard, and wire-rim glasses. A cop stops me as I leave the building to wander around and spend the twenty-five deutsche marks we Westerners are forced to change for each day we spend on the East side. He salutes smartly and announces, "*Ausweiss, bitte!*" — best translated as, "Your papers, please!"

I whip out my passport, and the deep blue book with the spread gold eagle does its trick. He knows right away that I'm no East German; he does not need to cross-examine me about my visit to the embassy. So he just makes a perfunctory check of my day visa and wishes me a *"schönen tag hier in Berlin,"* the German equivalent of "Have a nice day."

I make my way up the Unter den Linden, past the museums, the university, and the government buildings—all so quiet and empty compared with the bustle a few blocks away on the other side of the Wall, over the bridge across the Spree to the Centrum department store. The Centrum smells, and all the merchandise smells, like East Germany. West Germans say they can identify East Germans several ways. One is by the smell of their clothes. The centrally issued soap that's used throughout the country makes everything East smell like cheap disinfectant.

Centrum clothes look worse than the tackiest sale material at K-mart. There is nothing to consider buying, even as a joke. I head for the toys. I must spend the money; it's illegal to take it out of the country and worthless anywhere else anyway. I find a model Mig-21 and some Christmas cards in the stationery department. The cards are printed with fading colors on stiff and thick, poor-quality paper. They feel pulpy and rough. I grab an East German flag in the souvenir department, not guessing that it'll be a collector's item in a year, and leave myself enough of the aluminum change for a sandwich.

Waiting out in front of the store there is another reminder that this place isn't the people's paradise. Half a dozen shiny blue, official and brand-new Volvos are parked in a row. Their license plates, blue curtains, and goonlike chauffeurs mark the cars immediately to all the passing East German workers as belonging to the Communist Party hierarchy. Luxury Volvos are the cars of choice of the Communist leaders, and few other East Germans can get their hands on any Western cars, let alone such new and expensive models. The Volvos look so out of place on a street where the only other cars are the shabby little plastic Trabbies, toy-sized cars that cost the average worker over two years' salary and the ten-year wait.

I head back West, watching the changing of the guards — with their perfect goose steps — at the flame for the unknown soldier. All the official talk of antifascism in East Germany is surrounded not only by practicing fascists but also by all the fascist trappings, sullenly expressed by the grim young polished faces of those goose-stepping guards.

At Friedrichstrasse I spend the rest of my change on postcards and peanuts and get in line to get out of Commie-land. Next to me is a family with stacks of cardboard boxes. They are moving out of East Germany, hugging and kissing and crying their good-byes. My staring is caught by one of the crying women, and I feel the double standard again, my license, just because of that blue American passport, to observe others' unnecessary misery without sharing it.

But the show isn't over. I'm through the passport check and up on the platform waiting for the train back West. The Inter-shops here are open, selling Marlboros and Jacobs coffee and other Western goods for West marks at prices a few pfennigs less than in West Berlin. It's another of the curious and clever devices the East German government figured out to scrape together hard currency. West Berliners take the train one stop over the Wall for the discount shopping, a trip especially attractive to alcoholics pleased by the cheaper drink. When the drunks get too loud or obnoxious, East German police simply shove them into the next train West, slam the doors and dispatch the social problem across the border.

On the next platform over, border guards wait with two big black dogs. They look like a cross between German shepherds and pit bulls. Wire cages cover their jaws. A locomotive chugs in, and the engineer in his military-looking uniform acknowledges the dogs and guards. The locomotive is pulling a train heading West. It stops, and the guards and dogs climb on, routinely checking the engine for stowaways. The driver opens hatches; the guards shine flashlights.

What do they think? What occurs to them about such a bizarre job — searching a locomotive for people just trying to travel? And how did these guards rationalize their life's work, how did they put years of shooting their escaping neighbors into perspective, when just a few months later their work was made obsolete and they joined their enemy as one nation.

★   ★   ★

The Iron Curtain is rising. But let no one fool you; it is not gone. The legacy of a few generations of Stalinist authoritarian dictatorships cannot be wiped away by the remarkable 1989 revolutions. The damage to people, places, and things will last for at least a couple of generations.

Ironically, oppression by the Communists protected the European tribes under their control from traditional ethnic warring. Consequently, their new freedom is giving these disparate bands the opportunity to start killing each other again.

Once the Wall fell at the end of 1989, unification of the Germanys quickly began. I remember laughing about the commentaries I was reading from America that posed rhetorical questions about the possibility of unification. Those of us in Germany at that time knew there were no questions. We saw unification occurring almost immediately. We cringed at the headline in the right-wing newspaper *Deutsche Wochen-Zeitung*: "*Deutschland, Deutschland über alles, über alles in der Welt.*" The politicians were just rushing to catch up to the reality of unification with their new laws and approval. By the time the first meeting of the four World War II allies and the two Germanys convened in Bonn to take up the logistical problems of unification, the process itself was already irreversible.

Germans simply stopped recognizing the split and started interacting with each other as one people and one country again. There were many examples of this response, from the trivial to the consequential.

The party on the Wall lasted several days. Almost as soon as it was over, East Germans, taking advantage of their new right to travel freely, started pouring West in their smelly little Trabants and Wartburgs.[1] Plastered over their DDR country identifica-

---

[1]The Trabant was the East German Model T. It became familiar worldwide because so many East Germans escaped West through Hungary in their

tion stickers, they sported a variety of new alternatives. DDR is the abbreviation for what East Germany is called in German, the Deutsche Demokratische Republik. In English, the abbreviation is GDR, for German Democratic Republic. West Germany is known as the Bundesrepublik Deutschland. Some cars showed DDR stickers with the first D and the R struck out with red-colored slashes. Others incorporated the initials of both Germanys and read BRDDR. But most of the East Germans who changed their identity stickers simply slapped a standard D (for Deutschland) sticker over their DDR sticker, in spite of the fact that their cars were still registered in the DDR, still equipped with DDR license plates.

In a society as intent on following laws and orders as Germany's, this was a clear sign from the people that the days of a divided Germany were over.

West German entrepreneurs moved quickly to open the new market, taking advantage of the confusion of the revolutionary period. Officials in charge of regulations felt impotent, and opportunists moved in fast. Without waiting for any changes in the laws, they set up private shops in East cities. *Würst* stands sold sausages and West German beer on the sidewalks in Leipzig. News vendors in East Berlin sold previously forbidden West German magazines and newspapers from street corners. Events were moving so quickly during this revolutionary period that the government was forced to scramble just to catch up to reality as the people took advantage of the situation and decided for themselves what they wanted and how to get it.

And what they wanted, clearly, was what their West German cousins had: intellectual freedom and material wealth. That's why it shouldn't have been too much of a surprise to anyone when the election results were counted after the first free election in East Germany since Hitler took over.

Trabbies. The car was first manufactured in 1958, sports a plastic body and a two-cycle engine, and lunges for eighteen seconds getting from zero to twenty-five miles per hour. The most famous Trabbie joke: "Why is the rear window of the Trabbie heated? To keep your hands warm while you push it." The Wartburg is a slightly better car, also manufactured in the DDR.

The response was a complete rejection of the East German nation. "No more experiments," people told me. They voted overwhelmingly for a sure thing. They wanted to become West Germans. On the East side of what was left of the Berlin Wall, for the first time, graffiti started to sprout. In huge letters, someone scrawled, Germoney.

But who can argue with the East German voters and their decision? Certainly not those of us lucky enough to grow up and live with Western affluence. Even if we decide our life-styles are decadent and choose to reject them, we do that from the position of having had the opportunity to experience such prosperity. The East Germans, because of their unique relationship with West Germany, not only grew up poor and in bondage, but did it with a window facing their free, prosperous cousins. Every day as they struggled, they saw on West German TV, or when their relatives visited, exactly how it could have been for them. They saw how unnecessarily hard their existence was.

When freedom came, they saw the quickest likely route to a better life. They enjoyed an opening the other East bloc colonies did not, the chance to latch on to West Germany and its economic machine. Who can blame them for chucking their separate nation just as soon as they could? Even those who had the foresight to expect some of the problems unification is bringing had no stomach for any more unneeded struggle.

What the East Germans rejected was not socialism or communism. What they rejected was an oppressive dictatorship that hid behind the pretense of socialism by practicing some forms of it. It was a government that used guns to deny people basic human rights and creative opportunities.

On election day in East Germany in March 1990, I headed north out of Berlin into farming country and watched the voting in the crossroads of Wandlitz. The atmosphere was both festive and serious. Voters made their way to the polling place in a steady stream of motorbikes, bicycles, and smoking little cars, even on horseback.

The drill was simple. They showed their national identity cards, received their ballots, and disappeared into closets, built especially for the voting, where they secretly made their choices. Then volunteer election workers guided them to wooden strongboxes secured with padlocks, where the paper ballots were stored until the polls closed and the public counting started.

"This is German history!" one man told me proudly.

A young farmer came to vote for the Communists. He feared fast unification with West Germany. Upset about losing whatever good had come from the last forty years of building East Germany, he was convinced that there were positive aspects of the old system that could be retained without the East German people being oppressed by their leaders. He worried about East Germany being consumed and then taken advantage of by the West. But as he voted, he said he knew his party had no chance.

★ ★ ★

It was in Marx-Engels-Platz in Leipzig where the scream "*Wir sind ein Volk*" was first heard: "We are one people." Leipzig was the birthplace of the East German revolution. Quietly, months before the world considered that the East German government could possibly be overthrown, tiny groups of courageous dissidents gathered in the Saint Nikolai Church. After services that were combined with political meetings, they filtered out onto the streets to demonstrate peacefully against the government. The protesters, though often arrested, were not much noticed by the rest of the world.

Consider the newspapers in mid-June 1989, almost half a year before the Wall opened. The headlines were filled with Gorbachev's visit to Bonn. Less noticed were the stories about the twenty-five people arrested by the Stasi—the secret police—in Leipzig after taking part in a peace prayer at Saint Nikolai. They were stopped on their way from the church as they tried to march the few blocks to Marx-Engels-Platz.

This handful of demonstrators was a catalyst for the mass demonstrations a few months later that swept the government away. But between the time the Wall finally was punctured in November 1989, and the East German elections the next spring that led the way to unification, the crowds made it clear that German nationalism did not die with the Nazis.

I stood in the middle of hundreds of thousands of Leipzigers at one of those early Monday night demonstrations in November days after the Wall opened. It was dark. We had just left a packed service at Saint Nikolai, full of prayer and political lessons about human rights and the power of the people.

The pastor asked why the East Germany people — "who work as hard as the West German people" — shouldn't enjoy lives as free and successful as those of the West Germans. "People should have a chance," he taught, "to live freely with basic human rights." He cautioned against revenge, against violence, and then announced in a calm and nonthreatening manner, "The time of being oppressed is over."

The organ cranked up, and the congregation filled the church with the closing hymn. All the seats were taken; the aisles were packed. Some of the congregation were dressed in their best, others in grungy work clothes. Together they said the Lord's Prayer.

As the crowd left the church it was joined by others surging toward the Platz. This was before the government provided loudspeakers for the meetings. The organizers of the rally borrowed the equipment from a rock and roll band.

Spotlights played against the crowd and the mass of the facade of the opera house, its bulky Stalinist architecture just adding to the surreal mood. The dark, the spotlights, and the gray of the opera house made black and white the dominant colors of the evening.

The crowd yelled and cheered as one speaker after another made his or her way to the microphone to attack the government, and Erich Honecker and Egon Krenz personally.

"Krenz has a hundred thousand dollars in an American bank account!" called out an amplified voice from the podium. The crowd roared boos and whistled. There was an eerie lack of police; they stayed far back, gathered in twos and threes at the edge of the assembly.

It was a heady moment for the East Germans. Never before had anyone dared to charge into a microphone the challenges these speakers hurled at their dictators. They called them crooks who stole money from the people; they demanded freedoms for themselves, chanting "*Freiheit, freiheit.*"

The mob rage made some Leipzigers nervous. "Usually when there is a revolution, there is a party with a program leading it," a worried waiter told me that evening. "This time all the people went out in the street and forced the government out, but there is no plan for making a new government. The people want free elections, but how that will occur is unknown. That's why this is a chaotic, dangerous time."

The crowd chanted, "The Communist Party must go!" I looked around at a combination of concerned faces and excited joy.

A red-faced beggar stinking of liquor demanded a mark. I pulled out DDR money for him, and he rejected it. "No, I need West marks."

The revolution was clearly unstoppable. The people had let themselves loose, discovering their own power. "A hole in the Wall is not enough, Egon!" was a typical sign. People poked one another and pointed to the signs, repeating what the speakers were saying. It was like watching grammar school kids taking over the classroom while the teacher was out of the room. They couldn't quite believe that they were doing it, and now that they had started, they weren't going to stop.

Then that chant rolled through the crowd, filling the Platz: "*Wir sind ein Volk! Wir sind ein Volk!*"

The wild look in the eyes, the unison, the harshness of the syllables, the black-and-white lighting all conspired to evoke distinct memories of the hysterical "*Zieg Heil!*" from the crackly old black-and-white movies of Hitler's Nürnberg rallies.

★   ★   ★

Back in West Germany, on a drizzly, gray day in Bonn (there seem to be few days that aren't drizzly and gray in Bonn), I wandered into a startling display in the *fussgängerzone* — the downtown streets kept free of cars for wandering shoppers. At first it looked like just another street fair, the type that often fill the main squares in Germany offering food and games. But closer inspection showed that this was a fair with a theme and a political message: maintaining the German identity of lands that were no longer part of Germany, either East or West.

The food for sale was ethnic German stuff from regions no longer part of East or West Germany. The clothing was of the same ilk. So was the propaganda.

Typical was a flyer given out by an organization called Lands-mannschaft Schlesien—an organization arguing that Silesia must still be considered part of Germany. I picked up the English-language version of the pamphlet: "Silesia—a German Country." Inside is a map of Poland with those regions that were part of Germany before and during World War II shaded and marked "German eastern territories under Polish adminis-tration."[2]

Landsmannschaft Schlesien represents those Germans Chan-cellor Kohl was trying to mollify when he hesitated about guar-anteeing the Oder-Neisse Line as a permanent Polish-German border. They represent several million Germans who want to see lands in the east that Germany lost along with the war returned to the Fatherland. Their movement suffered a serious loss when Kohl and the unified Germany finally accepted the Polish border. But the cross-border nationalism these types of groups promote is something to worry about.

Germany continues, so many years after Hitler, to maintain an idea of citizenship that is very different from that of the United States. Being born in Germany gives a baby no right of citizenship. What makes a baby, or an adult, German is German blood pulsing through the body. Just how that blood is deter-mined to be German is specifically defined by current German law. Those Silesians or other Eastern Europeans who can show that somewhere along the family line their ancestors were Ger-man can just walk into Germany and enjoy, not only the full rights of citizenship, but all sorts of resettlement help. All they

---

[2]The curious can order their literature, which promotes a modern Germany with the borders it enjoyed back in 1937, from Landsmannschaft Schlesien, Nieder-und Oberschlesien e. V., Haus Schlesien, 5330 Königswinter 41, Germany.

need do is dig up the flimsiest of proof, a great-grandfather's army identity card, for example.

I watched at the Friedland refugee camp as a Polish family made their appeal to become West Germans. The wife did the talking; the husband's command of the German language was too poor. She told the investigating immigration officer some family stories and produced some tattered photographs of relatives looking German, along with some faded documents, and they were in. They got the stamp immediately making them members in good standing of the German Federal Republic. After a few more days in the dormitory of the camp, they would be off to a new life, leaving behind the economic and political uncertainties of Poland.

Meanwhile, Turkish workers who were seduced into coming to Germany years ago, back when their labor was needed, are being bribed to leave. At this point their communities include children and grandchildren of the original post-war Turkish work force. The government offers them cash buyouts if they forfeit any rights they've accumulated to German social service benefits, and they get a free plane ticket "back" to a Turkey they may be seeing for the first time.

With their citizenship law, Germans institutionalize and perpetuate the idea of a German race that is distinct from its neighbors and the rest of the world. As I traveled through Germany, I argued with Germans about their attempts to keep Germany for what they define as Germans. When I proposed the model of the American melting pot as a more appropriate alternative, especially during our era of easy mass travel, I was mocked. "Your melting pot is in your head," I was told over and over again. "America is not a happy, homogeneous society" is the sort of response I was subjected to. "The melting pot concept was tried and failed in America" is the widespread belief among Germans. "Instead, you're left with a nation filled with separate and fighting ethnic groups," they insist.

But it is the German model of trying to preserve some sort of ethnic purity that doesn't work. Germany is already an immigrant nation, yet many Germans fight that reality and do not want to share the benefits of being German with newcomers lacking a good German pedigree. By discouraging immigrants from seeking citizenship, Germany is creating a restive under-class. It is a policy that will only lead to future conflicts.

Over lunch a few months before the Wall opened, the minis-ter-president of Rheinland-Pfalz, Dr. Bernhard Vogel, was quite unbelievably candid for a German politician as we talked about the East German immigrants who were filling up his state. He welcomed them because they were Germans, were likely to vote for his conservative party, and were ready to work.

Yes, he readily admitted, he'd much rather have a German doing his dirty work than a Turk.

Germany is not alone with this chauvinistic attitude. The future stability of post-Communist Eastern Europe relies on the people coming to terms with their varied ethnic backgrounds and developing some sort of process for peaceful coexistence.

★   ★   ★

By the end of 1990, Saddam Hussein and his invasion of Kuwait solved a nasty problem for both Germany and America: what to do with the hundreds of thousands of American army troops and their masses of materiel stuffed into West Germany. Most of them, and much of the East German army's Soviet-built equipment, were shipped off to the Persian Gulf. The new enemy and the new assignment probably provided some psycho-logical relief for the confused soldiers who had spent forty-five years on alert along the Iron Curtain, waiting to scramble and stop the invading Warsaw Pact army that never came over the border.

One of the first changes in the lives of American soldiers after the East German government opened the Iron Curtain was the new rule about acknowledging the presence of the soldier on the other side. It became permissible to wave at those who had been adversaries for so long, but only if the other guy waved first.

There was at least one ecstatic soldier, as the Iron Curtain opened. American Private Arnold Kephart stumbled out of East Germany, thirty years after he deserted the American forces. In 1960, poor Private Kephart, just twenty-three years old, was assigned to drive an army truck from France back to his base at Heidelberg. As Private Kephart tells the story, he and his buddies bought a few bottles of wine to bring back from France. They crashed the truck.

"In the crash, the wine got broke up on our uniforms," Kephart told a reporter thirty years later. "The police, they thought we had been drunk. We didn't have one single drink from the wine," he still insisted. But they were arrested and the army told them that they would be sent to prison and forced to pay for the wrecked truck.

Instead, Private Kephart escaped, and on the advice of a girlfriend ran to East Germany. There he started a new life. But it was not a happy life, and he tried to come home. He was trapped, not allowed to leave East Germany, unable to escape until the border opened.

At first the American army arrested him, but then they decided to let him go, and he returned to Omaha saying, "I'm going to live it up first, and then I'm going to sit down and try to work my way in life." Now fifty-three, before ducking out of the public spotlight Private Kephart announced, "I don't know how I'm going to say it, but I'll say I'm proud to be back in the United States."

For the German border towns that relied on Allied armies for much of their financial strength, the sudden loss of American soldiers was a serious worry, but it was a concern offset by confidence that the strong German economy would soon compensate for the loss. There was good news for the Germans, too. The quick disappearance of the Allies meant the end of stockpiled weapons and low-level jet fighter practice flights. And it meant that land used by the armies could be turned over to civilian uses.

★   ★   ★

The real military losers after the Iron Curtain parted were the Soviet soldiers and their families stationed in East Germany. Not only were they a hated occupation army, they were suddenly broke, with nothing but a bleak future facing them once they were sent home. Once the deutsche mark took over the economy of what is now called just eastern Germany, the purchasing power of Soviet soldiers' pay plummeted to nearly nothing.

Soldiers and their wives started looting the bases and their own homes, selling whatever they could get their hands on. The Brandenburg Gate and Checkpoint Charlie turned into impromptu flea markets filled with Soviet military paraphernalia.

"You want one of these hats, hon?" the loud American voices reverberate under the Brandenburg Gate. Tourists model not just Soviet but also old East German army hats and whole uniforms that are for sale. There are hammer-and-sickle pins, special commemorative Lenin pins, badges from the Young Pioneers, political philosophy books, flags and banners. The giggling Western tourists survey the remnants of the suddenly finished empire, capitalist victors picking through the totems of the failed society, enjoying the symbolic spoils of the vanquished without even fighting the war.

One miserable-looking group of older Soviet women stands grimly in the cold, selling Soviet officers' watches, samovars, Russian dolls, bottles of Russian vodka.

Rumors fill the streets that Kalashnikovs and all sorts of weapons are available in addition to the souvenirs. One of the vendors, a Greek middleman, tells me he's convinced it's not true, that he would be able to get them if they were on the market. But a friend of mine is blasting around the streets of Berlin on his new East German army motorcycle, still painted in the dirty official green. He bought it for just a few hundred dollars and guarantees me anything manufactured by the East German government is available at a bargain price.

I sense a sadness, certainly not nostalgia for the oppressive ways of the losers, but regret over the lives wasted building their bankrupt society and disgust at the crass manners of the victors picking through the remains.

An organ grinder cranks out *blass musik* — the oom-pah-pah band music; *würst* and ice-cream hawkers sell their wares; TV crews take pictures. It is the eve of the official unification party, but the atmosphere is not festive; it carries little of the emotional euphoria I felt at the same spot a year before as the crowds celebrated the Wall opening. I feel, instead, the galloping West arrogantly, carelessly staking its claim. Unification is really West Germany consuming East Germany while the East Germans are preoccupied consuming the products of West Germany. But as the icons of the losers are reduced to flea market junk, more and more Germans question the speedy merger.

Behind the celebratory fireworks, speeches, and patriotic music that mark unification is a long haul toward any real unity. The systems, cultures, and people that have developed so separately since World War II cannot just immediately become one.

Left behind as East Germany disappears into the eastern part of a united Germany are the revolutionaries who were on the front lines just a year before, gathering in the tiny groups, sure to be arrested and persecuted. The role they played in forcing the totalitarian regime out of business is virtually ignored. Instead Chancellor Kohl and his center-right political party are seizing credit for unification, with Kohl leading the parade knowing he'll now go down in history as the leader who brought Germany together, ended the occupation of Berlin, and restored full sovereignty to Germany. The rush to abandon a separate East Germany leaves plenty of questions: Will the East Germans' get-rich-quick dream come true, or will they become second-class citizens of a united Germany's poor and neglected eastern region?

They've lost their cradle-to-grave job and social security, traded away the possibility of maintaining not only a separate identity, but also some sort of socialist government without the oppression of totalitarian communism. Will they regret their cavalier rejection once they tire of their new Western toys?

A West Berlin newspaper cartoon suggests there are no regrets and the transition is smooth. A boss in the first panel is coming to work the day before unification. *"Guten Morgen, Genossedirektor,"* says the guard at the door, "Good morning, comrade director." The next day, after unification, the same guard tells the same boss, *"Grüss Gott, Herr Geschäftsführer,"* a Western greeting to the boss he now calls "Mr. Business

Leader." The cartoon shows unification bringing together people with substantially different mentalities, but it's not such an easy task in real life.

Differences in language and dress make it easy for the urbane Westerners to pick out their often unsophisticated cousins. Over the years, the East Germans' vocabulary filled up with awkward and forced-sounding words. These additions came from their government's propaganda, like the title comrade. In East Germany, the more neutral-tone *Kamerad* was replaced by the highly politicized variant *Genosse*. Other words come from their nation's superpower affiliation: they say cosmonaut not astronaut, for example. Their clothing is either the cheap sameness of denim and plastic from government factories or styles imported from the West that the elite Westerners call "new chic." Hip Westerners reject the overdressed "new chic" look in favor of jeans and a sweater or more traditional styles.

This cultural separation creates an aloofness in the Westerners toward the Easterners. A friend of mine who owns a swank West Berlin restaurant summed up what he sees as the prevailing Western attitude, "For forty-five years we said, 'Please come.' And now that they're free we say, 'We don't need you for propaganda. Stay away.' It's our arrogance."

The Easterners feel the loss and rebuff. I spent an afternoon with two East German colleagues just as their nation was being dissolved. These were professional men, radio broadcasters who made decent money. We were driving around in their older, but adequate, car, saving the disappearing images with an older, but adequate, home video tape recorder. We took pictures of what was left of the Checkpoint Charlie border station. The room where I had been held and interrogated had been vandalized, the sink ripped off the wall, the windows broken. We walked along the border where the Wall had divided the city at Bernauerstrasse. The guard tower had already been knocked down along this stretch of the Wall where Berliners were killed trying to escape the East through old houses. Then we stopped for a fancy cake and coffee at the brand-new and private Grenzenlos

Café on the East side. The name of the café is appropriate; it means borderless. We were tourists together.

"Hungary changed its government; Poland changed its government," mused one of my companions, Thomas Frohn. "But Hungary is still Hungary; Poland is still Poland. We've become strangers in our own land."

★   ★   ★

Lying just on the West side of the old border between the two Germanys, Duderstadt looks the way Germany is supposed to look. Especially contrasted with the gritty frontier city that is Berlin, or sleazy, Americanized Frankfurt, Duderstadt is quaint and cute. Perfectly restored and maintained, it is filled with half-timbered houses, picturesque churches — and a swastika-desecrated memorial to the destroyed Jewish temple.

Before the Iron Curtain rose, the West German government ran tours from Duderstadt to see the horrors of the East German border. First came a briefing at the army outpost, explaining the German-German border fortifications constructed by the DDR. The West German army officer described the fences, the spotlights, the guard towers, the dog runs, the automatic machine guns, the barbed wire. Then we all climbed on board a bus to go take a look for ourselves. It was, perhaps, a more eerie sight than the Berlin Wall cutting through the city.

Here was the barrier between the two German states bisecting open countryside. The bucolic setting, the rolling green hills were perversely disturbed by harsh concrete and steel. At one point near Duderstadt, the boundary headed directly toward a medieval village. When the dice were rolled, this village went to the DDR, so the border fencing took a berserk path around the sad-looking village, hugging it inside East Germany. So close to sparkling Duderstadt, the East German village is drab and quiet.

The German-German border followed old provincial lines, so the fence path was rarely straight. It wandered idiotically, taking inexplicable turns in the middle of nowhere, often at right angles, creating impenetrable corners in sprawling pastures.

The craziness was not limited to the East side. I heard barking dogs and looked over to see men quickly taking positions with their rifles on the West side. They were spread out, back from the border barrier, cordoning off a corner. But they were not soldiers. It took a minute to figure out what was going on—men in place, dogs running, jumping, barking, rifles at the ready. And then I saw the deer. These were West German hunters, operating en masse, using the Iron Curtain to corral game into their gunsights.

*   *   *

About an hour east of pristine Duderstadt, back across the border on the East side, is one of the East German government's lasting legacies. Along with ruined lives, the postwar years leave a toxic scorched earth. To travel to Bitterfeld is to see environmental catastrophe. I watched as a shift changed and the workers trudged back and forth across the street between their houses and the factory. The air stank of chemicals; from smokestacks lining the horizon, clouds of yellow ochre poison pumped and billowed into the sky. The trees were stunted, dead and dying. A skull and crossbones on a sign at a stagnant lake warned against swimming and fishing. The swill lying on the water surface looked so grimy, it was difficult to imagine anyone considering a swim, sign or no sign.

The negative image of what is now the eastern part of Germany will be hard for the region to shake. Right down the road from Bitterfeld, Halle is trying with devices like a full-page advertisement in the *London Financial Times* that insists, "*Halle hat Zukunft.*" The choice of words reflects either a poor copywriter or a pleading attitude. *Halle hat Zukunft* literally means "Halle has future." Perhaps it could be loosely interpreted as meaning Halle has a future. Either way, it calls for new investors in the city from a position of wishful thinking. It's hard to imagine a Western city that couldn't come up with a much more insistent slogan, like "Halle is the future."

Halle's trepidation is understandable, considering not only the ruined land but also the miserable economic statistics in eastern Germany a year after the border opened. Industrial production was falling and unemployment rising, while the territory of the old West Germany continued to report increasing production and growing employment.

★   ★   ★

Among those looking for new jobs were East Germany's diplomats. I ran into one at a conference in Mississippi, the press attaché at the Washington embassy, Frank Mader. He was coping as well as could be expected with his uncertain future. "I'm trained as a journalist," he told me, suggesting he could just slide from his foreign ministry career into news reporting. I gently reminded him that his journalism training in the DDR — basically lessons in toeing the Party line — hardly qualified him for the free press coming to his old country. He nodded numbly, but his mood picked up considerably when he started talking about his coming vacation. He was equipped with a rented car. After the conference and before his trip back to Germany he was seeing America.

He worried about his reception back home, telling a reporter just before he left Washington, "Of course, there are some people in the government who have not worked for the interests of the people. I believe such people should go on trial. But there are some other people who really believed in the system. I hope such people don't face hostility from others." He was talking about himself, of course. "I hope people will see how we worked."

A year after the East German communist government fell, *The European* newspaper managed to interview Erich Honecker, an interview Honecker's lawyers quickly criticized as full of inaccuracies and based on a private conversation. Honecker spoke in the Soviet military hospital where he was living under house arrest. It was the first detailed public analysis of the changes in Germany to come from him since the Wall opened. He explained his position to an old colleague from his days in the anti-Nazi resistance, Heinz Junge.

Honecker denied living a life of luxury. "It is a great disappointment to me that so many people have forgotten socialism and turned to the D-mark instead. In the end I will be seen to have been right. It has already become quite obvious to all what rights and social services they have lost."

Photographs that accompanied the interview showed Honecker looking drawn and somber. He wore an open-necked blue shirt, the same light blue his photographers had for the background of his official pictures. "I consider all the charges so far brought by the prosecutor's office to be untenable. I also reject responsibility for the figure, cited by the prosecutor's office, of two hundred killed on the DDR borders. I have no personal guilt for that. And what, I ask myself, about those who killed DDR border guards while violating our frontiers?" It was Honecker who engineered the construction of the Berlin Wall in 1961.

Honecker remained defiant in the interview. "The communist movement has suffered a defeat, but will recover," he said, adding that he expects to participate in that recovery. "I will fight on."

Chapter Three

BERLIN WALL-LESS

"We're making the Wall go away!"
— West German grammar school kids chipping away
at the Wall with hammers,
dancing around the falling concrete chips, November 1989

BROWN COAL SMOKE lingers in the Berlin air. Brown coal, the soft coal that's easy to mine in Eastern Europe, burns dirty and shortens the life span of those forced to breathe it. The smell is sweet, the fallout filthy, covering streets and buildings with black grit. Cars get so dirty after a few weeks, the soot won't come off in an automatic car wash.

The Berlin sky is usually gray even without the brown coal. Perhaps the foul weather adds to the angst-ridden mentality of the Germans. But my artist friend Dagmar complains that she tires of the few sunny days that run together in the late summer. She looks forward to the gray. It soothes her.

In the summer of 1988, my family and I moved into a flat in Moabit, a working-class district, populated with a combination of poor Germans, students, and Turks. As in most of Berlin, the apartment building was unadorned, drab and without color. On the street level was a closed-up bar, the So Wie So — the Anyway.

The building entrance door was translucent glass, with wire mesh running through it, in an aluminum frame. A flight of stairs led up to the tiny elevator. The first couple of floors were filled with doctor's offices. Grotesquely sick old Germans painfully made their way up the stairs. Even if they used the elevator, they were forced to go up and down stairs. Because of the way

the elevator was added to the building, it only stopped on the
landings between floors.

I painted out the graffiti in the elevator with a cheery blue. In
just a few days it was back: swastikas, *"Nazis Raus!"* and "I gone
be a dirty punk." I painted it out a couple more times before
giving up.

One of the surprises of living in Germany was the constant
reminders of the Nazis. I expected to be thinking of the Nazi
time myself, but seeing how much a part of modern West
Germany it remains was disconcerting.

After we rented our flat we learned that the apartment
building was one of many in Berlin owned by the Munich
publisher and politician Gerhard Frey. It was one of Frey's
newspapers that featured the post-Wall headline *"Deutschland,
Deutschland über alles, über alles in der Welt."* Another of his
papers is called the *Deutsche National Zeitung*—the German
National Newspaper. The typography evokes the tone of Nazi
propaganda. A harsh cross fits neatly between *National* and
Zeitung on the paper's nameplate.

"Is Frey a neo-Nazi?" I asked a German journalist friend after
seeing the papers.

"No," was the answer, "he's an old Nazi."

Skinheads in Berlin celebrated Hitler, marching around with
their arms stretched out in the Nazi salute. *Mein Kampf* was still
outlawed; only recognized scholars who could show a need to
know were allowed to possess Hitler's book.[1]

From the front rooms of the flat I could see the Woolworth's
sign on Turmstrasse, a shopping strip without much European
charm and romance. It looked like an American rust-belt main
drag: supermarkets, drugstores, the Woolworth's, cheap shoe

---

[1] A brief, minor scandal hit in late 1988 when a television reporter stumbled on
Mein Kampf for sale at the Stars and Stripes bookstore at the American army
PX in Berlin. The book was immediately pulled from the shelves, raising
questions of free speech for the Americans stationed in the still-occupied city.
A postwar Allied law prohibiting the distribution of material spreading racial
hatred was cited when the book was removed from the store.

stores. German coffee houses and Turkish kabob stands added just a touch of color.

The back view out of the apartment was of trash cans in the concrete courtyard and a glimpse of sky. We were on the top floor. Around the corner was a fire station. Roosting pigeons took the edge off the fire engine sirens with their cooing. Berlin is a vibrant city; it is not pretty.

Much of the bomb damage was quickly replaced in the fifties and sixties with perfunctory boxes; the painstaking restoration seen in other parts of Germany is missing from most of Berlin.

I lived in Moabit for the year before the Communist governments in Eastern Europe started collapsing. The Wall was a constant presence, just a few blocks away. It was always offensive, this assault on free movement, but there were amusing encounters with the Wall now and again.

One winter day two Polish car thieves were racing away from West Berlin police. They tried to escape through the Bornholmerstrasse border crossing point. The East German border guards rejected them and sent them back West, where they were arrested. West Berlin, surrounded by the Wall, was a bad place for a run from the police.

When the Wall opened, it was bad news for some cheating West Berlin husbands who had managed to acquire East Berlin girlfriends. East Berlin lovers were inexpensive for West Berlin men, who crossed the border equipped with powerful deutsche marks. But there was another valuable benefit to picking an East Berliner for a mistress. The Wall made it pretty unlikely wife and girlfriend would ever meet.

*   *   *

Just hours after the Berlin Wall was breached in November 1989, I was on board a Lufthansa 747 heading back to Germany from San Francisco.

"Are you going over to celebrate?" asked the reservations clerk, as she booked my seat.

German-born Ilka Hartmann was going for the party.

"I was there, sixteen years old, when the Wall was built," she told me as the jet climbed over the Golden Gate Bridge. She had decided the night before to take time off from work and fly to her homeland. "I just felt I was in the wrong part of the world at the moment." She arranged a week-long leave and raced to the airport.

"I felt a burden falling off us Germans. I never expected in our lifetime there might be a possibility of the two Germanys coming together."

As the plane headed east, she talked of the Berlin Wall as a pain that she had carried with her since 1961. "It seemed like a punishment for German history. It feels like the war is really over for me." Smiling, laughing, talking so fast the words spilled out, both German and English, she kept saying, "Unbelievable!"

It was a word spoken over and over again in both languages on the overnight flight.

San Francisco State University graduate student Mark Beinner was another passenger who couldn't sleep on that flight. "I woke up this morning and turned on CNN and said, 'I'm going!' It's history in the making, just like the earthquake."

Beinner saw the Berlin Wall for the first time when he was stationed in Germany during service in the U.S. Army.

"I want to grab a piece of the Wall and take it back," he announced to anyone who would listen. "I want to be able to put that on my shelf and look at it and say, 'That is something that was overcome by the people.' It was keeping people from doing what they wanted."

The plane was filled with astounded Germans reading the latest newspapers. The headline in the conservative paper *Die Welt* proclaimed: "The German people are the happiest people in the world!"

The years of oppressive Stalinist rule in East Germany seemed to make most people forget why Germany was split. It was divided because Germany lost a war it started and the victors concluded that the aggressor would be less of a future menace if carved into smaller pieces. Then the United States and the rest of the Western Allies decided that the new threat was Communism and the Soviet Union. Convinced that the Soviet empire was permanent, the Allies found it easy to make eventual German unification a publicly stated policy goal. The unspoken, but commonly accepted, conclusion in the West always was that the Soviets would never relinquish or lose their East German colony. Consequently, the West could claim eventual German unification as a lofty goal, knowing the Soviets would never allow it to happen.

Western, especially American, policymakers made two short-sighted errors with that theory.

The first was to believe their own propaganda. They convinced themselves that the Communist threat was so potent that East Germany would always be ruled by Moscow. Gorbachev, and the street demonstrations that led to the collapse of the Wall, proved them wrong.

Their second mistake was to reinforce the idea that the Germanys are pushed by some sort of moral, historical, and necessary force to be one political entity. But unification was not imperative. Two German states could have existed separately after the Wall fell.

The Soviets and their puppets abused East Germany. The oppression in the German Democratic Republic was an unacceptable continuation of many of the crimes of the Nazis. But the alternative need not have been a united Germany.

The naive policy of the Western Allies, always expecting the Soviets to prevent the unification that the Allies endorsed, combined with the oppressive regime installed by the Soviets, created an ideal climate for German nationalists. They were able to convince the world that German unification was inevitable and appropriate.

Not all Germans bought the unification arguments. The writer Günter Grass maintained up to the end that there were better alternatives. In a speech after the Wall opened, Grass tried to remind West Germans how long and hard East Germans suffered from the Nazi crimes and their aftermath. "No sooner had the Greater German system of tyranny lost its power," said Grass, "than the Stalinist system closed in, with new yet familiar forms of tyranny. Economically exploited by a Soviet Union that had previously been exploited and devastated by the Greater German Reich, confronted immediately with Soviet tanks during the workers' uprising in June 1953, and finally walled in, the citizens of the German Democratic Republic had to pay, and pay and pay again, on their own behalf as well as on the behalf of the citizens of the Federal Republic. They unfairly bore the brunt of the Second World War, which had been lost by all Germans."

Grass believed some sort of confederation of the two German states was needed, both to preserve the separate identity established by the East Germans and to spare the world the dangers of a united Germany.

★   ★   ★

But the East Germans, so long denied basic human rights and the affluent life-style enjoyed by their cousins in the West, were primed to throw away the separate identity they had created since the end of the war.

The West Germans, too, were enthralled with the idea of union. It appealed to their latent — and not always so latent — nationalism. It appealed to their pocketbooks, too. Here was a cheap labor pool to drive a continuing German economic boom. But this time the workers were from the same roots, spoke the same language. West Germans accelerated their efforts to get rid of Turkish workers they had imported to do the hard and dirty work.

Turks in West Berlin immediately saw the arriving East Berliners as a threat to their livelihood. Already discriminated against because of their Muslim religion, worry beads, and garlic-filled food, the Turks now feared for their jobs in Germany.

Sipping tea in a falafel shop just a few blocks from a new hole in the Wall, Turkish-born engineer Hakkam Yavus searched for the right English words. "The people from East Germany have the same culture as the people here," he said slowly. "There will be prejudice against the Turkish people because East German people need work and houses."

On another flight back to Europe just a few months after the Wall opened, I sat next to a medical student on his way home to Germany. He had taken a breather from his studies and traveled through the United States and Latin America. He had been away during all the radical changes back in Germany. So what did he think?

"I don't relate to the state."

He glanced at the *International Herald Tribune* I was reading and grunted at the headline that reported: "Kohl's plea: Trust the new Germany."

"Don't," he urged.

"A lot of people are worried," I said.

"They should be," was his curt response.

★ ★ ★

One of my lingering and recurring concerns is the transformation of the East German border guards and cops from murdering storm troopers to smiling recipients of flowers from cute girls. The pictures flashed around the world. Taking a cue from Berkeley in the sixties, the fräuleins stuck the flowers down gun barrels.

But there was an important difference. The East German soldiers were practicing hired killers, shooting their own escaping citizens one day, grinning and accepting flowers the next. This was the same army that shot and killed eighteen-year-old Peter Fechter back in 1962, in what was to become one of the saddest examples of the East German attitude toward escapees. Fechter was not killed when he was hit by border patrol fire, just wounded. He had climbed over the first wire fence on the East side, made a dash through the cleared land on the east side of the Wall known as the death strip, and been hit by DDR bullets just as he was getting to the Wall itself. He screamed and fell bleeding. The West police threw him first aid supplies but did not violate their interpretation of the complicated agreements on Berlin and cross the Wall to help the dying man. The Communists just watched too, until finally Fechter bled to death.

The shootings continued until just before the Wall came down. I didn't keep track of all the attacks on escaping East Germans that occurred while I lived in Berlin, just enough of them to remind me about the work of the border guards, the newspeak-named *Volkspolizei* — people's police. From the British Military Government and the U.S. mission I received a daily press summary and review. Some samples from just a few months before the Wall came down include this from February 7, 1989:

> Shots from GDR border guards late on Sunday evening prevented an escape by a man who attempted to scale the Wall in Neuköln. Ten shots were fired. The man was eventually dragged away to a waiting vehicle and driven away. Reports indicate the man may have been shot and possibly killed during the incident.

Another I saved was from April 8, 1989:

> East German border guards used their firearms yesterday to prevent an escape attempt at the border crossing point of Chausseestrasse in Berlin's Wedding district. The incident involved two young men, and both were seen being arrested.

On June 21, 1989, was this sad story:

> The case of a would-be escapee is on the front pages of *Tagesspiegal*, *Morgenpost* and *Volksblatt*. It involves one Martin Notev, who attempted to escape across the river Spree near the Reichstag. He reached Western territory in the British sector of west Berlin clinging to the stone-clad river bank with one hand, when an east Berlin patrol boat appeared, into which Herr Notev was dragged. One east Berlin officer was seen actually with one foot on Western territory. Notev has since been sentenced to four years imprisonment and a fine of 40,000 marks.

That same day included this note:

> Allied circles revealed yesterday that east Berlin was making increasing use of packs of dogs at the Wall to prevent escapes, with the animals running along the boundary on long leads. It is not known whether this signals a curtailment of the order to shoot would-be escapees.

I had irritating experiences with the border guards, too. They weren't shooting at me, but we weren't exchanging flowers either.

At Checkpoint Charlie in 1987 I was locked in a holding cell for several hours one day as I was returning to West Berlin from the East side. I was working on a report about the origin of the story that AIDS was the result of a runaway CIA experiment, and I had traced the story back to what appeared to be its source, an old East German university professor living out his retirement in a high-rise apartment near the Wall.

With my satchel full of notes from the interview and a tape recorder, I walked back toward the border crossing. The guard-house sat like some sort of misguided, oversized tollbooth right up on the line that separates East and West. That's what it was for many years, a tollbooth. The East Germans charged curious tourists five marks for a day visa to enter the country in addition to the twenty-five West German marks spending money they were forced to exchange for twenty-five of the vastly less valuable East German marks. It was like an admission ticket to the Communist Disneyland.

Paranoia was built into the design of the passport control office. The officer in charge sat up above the passageway you were forced to make your way through, looking down through a glass window in his cage. Your way was blocked by the solid, locked door. The area was lit up brightly with irritating fluorescent tubes. A mirror placed at a forty-five-degree angle above the guard made it possible for him to see in your back pockets.

The drill was always stern — no smiles or casual exchanges as he took your passport, looked at the visa and your picture, then studied your face to make sure you were you. Then the procedure was repeated, to make really sure.

If all your papers were in order, the solid, imitation-wood, metal door buzzed. The lock was now open and you passed into the customs inspection zone. Usually this was the end of what the Germans call *Pass Kontrolle*. But for whatever reason, on this trip, the customs officer decided to take a look in my bag.

"*Vertrauen ist gut,*" goes the German saying, "*aber Kontrolle ist besser.*" "Trust is good, but control is better."

When he found the cassette recorder, I was charged with practicing journalism without a proper permit and led into the holding room. My bag and papers were taken, the door was locked, and I was left.

The room was empty except for a desk and a couple of chairs. There was, bizarrely, a washbasin, too, and a row of coat hooks. There was one window. The glass was frosted. Through it I could hear the murmur of returning tourists as they lined up for *Kontrolle*.

Periodically, one guard or another would come back with some scrap from my papers and we'd converse briefly.

"What's this?"

"A credit card receipt for gasoline."

And he'd be gone again.

Finally my stuff was returned intact, and I was allowed through to the West side after being cautioned to get approval before I attempted another reporting job in the East. The fact that the professor I had interviewed on my forbidden tape recorder was part of their propaganda machine probably speeded up my release.

The other crossing point for Westerners into East Berlin was the Friedrichstrasse train station. Both the subway and the elevated trains entered the East sector from the West there, where the *Kontrolle* apparatus blocked the entrance to the street. As late as January 1989 I came walking through carrying a copy of the *International Herald Tribune*.

"This is not allowed in the German Democratic Republic," an irritated guard informed me, pulling it from my hand. He walked me over to a garbage can and told me to dump it, making an overt public display indicating that he was not just confiscating it himself to take home.

Then I was escorted to a windowless cubicle and told to empty my pockets.

"What's this, hashish or heroin?" The guard was fingering pocket lint that clung to my wallet.

Again, credit card slips were fascinating to the inspector.

This time the delay was only a few irritating minutes.

So the overnight conversion of the people's police from murderers to good guys was difficult for me to accept. Yet, right after the Wall opened in November 1989, I was milling with the crowd at the Brandenburg Gate. The border guards were patrolling on top of the Wall, by this time keeping the celebrating Berliners off of it. A West Berliner yelled up to one of the cops, "Please give me a piece for my garden wall!"

The policeman responded, "I thought we wouldn't build any more walls."

The crowd cheered. He smiled.

A few yards away, between the Brandenburg Gate and the Reichstag, revelers passed a stark wooden cross. It commemorates Heinz Sokolowski, who was shot November 1965, trying to escape from East Berlin. As Berliners celebrated the new openings in the Wall and the announcement that the entire border between the two Germanys would no longer be a free-fire zone for the East Germany border guards, Heinz Sokolowski was not forgotten.

Fresh flowers covered the ground at the base of the cross; candles burned there, too. Berliners strolled by enjoying the glow of the moment and stopped and looked, some taking pictures of this man's memorial, a man shot dead for doing what millions had done in the last few days: cross the artificial line between the two Berlins.

On the West side, the first days after the Wall opened, the West Berlin police found themselves in the curious role of keeping people away from the Wall.

"It's not allowed," explained a West policeman chasing away a souvenir hunter. "The Wall belongs to the German Democratic Republic, and they don't like it when someone from West Germany tries to break the Wall."

Those first hours and days after the Wall opened, the worry was that something might trigger terrible violence amid the celebrations. But there were not enough police to prevent the souvenir hunters from chipping away at the barricade, and the party was over for the East German Communists anyway. They just looked on as hammers, pipes, and rocks were used to whack away at the Wall for chips.

Before, "We didn't talk together," said the West Berlin cop looking up at the Volkspolizei. "They are people, we are people; I think we have to work together. They are East German."

He was pondering the same question: How could the Volks-polizei change overnight? "They are East German," he worked on it, "but they are German. We are also German, so now it is somewhat equal to be East or West. It doesn't matter."

*   *   *

A year after the Wall opened, it was still not exactly clear who had decided to open the Wall. The best evidence suggests it was not a single order but a series of miscalculations that combined fortuitously with the East Germans aching to see the West.

The East German Communist government was panicking as it fell apart. The end started during the summer of 1989, as the Hungarians continued their measured walk away from Commu-nism by cutting down their barbed wire stretch of the Iron Curtain. The result was not just symbolic. Thousands and thousands of vacationing East Germans suddenly realized they could just drive their smoking Trabbies west out of Hungary to a new life in West Germany instead of going back home to a lifetime of drudgery and worse.

Then East Germans who weren't on vacation figured out that they could gain their freedom with the same route, by just hopping in their cars and driving through Czechoslovakia to Hungary. They watched on West German television as the ecstatic refugees were greeted by friendly West Germans; they saw the videotape of the lines of Trabbies going West.

Over the next few months the demonstrations by East Ger-mans who wanted to stay spread from Leipzig to most other East German cities. Erich Honecker was dumped by the Party and replaced by his right-hand man, Egon Krenz. According to news reports in the *Washington Post* and *Der Spiegal*, govern-ment spokesman Günter Schabowski had ended up with in-complete information at his November 9 press conference. After a day of behind-the-scenes scrambling by the government to come up with a plan to slow the exodus of its citizens,

Schabowski was told to read a message about changing travel regulations.

"Private trips abroad can be applied for," Schabowski read. "Permits will be granted promptly." The idea, apparently, was to slow the embarrassing public race out of the country by convincing people they could travel normally in the future.

But the note was without detail. In what form must these trips be applied for? How fast is "promptly"?

The problem was complicated further when nobody in the foundering East German government bothered to tell the West Germans, the Soviets, the Allies still occupying and administering West Berlin, or even — unbelievably — the East German border guards about what appeared to be a radical policy change.

But as soon as the news hit the public, Schabowski's words were interpreted as meaning East Germans could finally go wherever they wanted to go whenever they wanted to go there. And they swarmed by the thousands toward the gates of the Berlin Wall.

Border guards were forced to make a quick decision: open up or start shooting? Krenz later wrote an explanatory article for *Der Spiegal* saying that the guards had called party leaders for advice and he, Krenz, had ordered the border opened. Because deposed leaders like Krenz labored quickly to save their lives and their places in history, the true chronology of November 9, 1989, may never be assembled. *Neues Deutschland*, the official newspaper of the East German Communist Party as the Wall opened, reported a year later — when it was no longer a government-controlled paper — that two Stasi officials had given the order to open the Wall, not Krenz.

What is clear is that the power of the press of people forced the Wall open, no matter who gave the appropriate order not to shoot.

The party and the vigil at the Wall lasted for several days, on through the weekend, as Berliners — West and East — took a look for themselves, making sure it was not just a dream.

"Yesterday I heard you are going to tear down the Wall," one suggested to a border guard.

"Anything is possible," answered the Volpo — the Volkspolizei.

Usually the gray weather of oncoming winter adds to the sour faces and grim attitudes of Germans in public. There's little smiling in the streets. But the euphoria after the Wall opened extended for days; casual conversations started spontaneously among strangers, certainly common back home in California, but just about unknown in Berlin.

"It's just like Christmas," said one German friend who felt forced to explain the out-of-character frivolity.

"New Year's, Christmas, and everything all together," said another.

At a coffee and juice bar I frequented near the Europa Center, the owner was all smiles early in the morning as he told me he was out of sugar and out of oranges because of the "unbelievable weekend."

The line for newspapers was long at the Zoo Station newsstand; East Germans could buy papers still unavailable blocks away just across the border, and now could just carry them home. Censorship became irrelevant and impossible as soon as the border opened. One headline in the scandal sheet *Bild* was printed with the letters colored black, red, and yellow to look like the German flag. It yelled, *"Guten Morgen Deutschland."* On that same front page was a telegram that the right-wing newspaper had sent to Gorbachev: "You've made Germany happy, Mr. Gorbachev. We thank you."

★ ★ ★

Most of the visitors went home after a look around. Mathias Kromphardt was one of the day tourists, but he kept coming back for more. I pulled him out of the stream passing through the gate on Invalidenstrasse at the Sandkrugbrücke. He was wearing the typical plastic windbreaker and cheap-looking pre-faded jeans. We talked on the West side. This was the British sector, and smiling British soldiers offered hot coffee from a military canteen to the hoards making their way through the chilly Berlin air. The soldiers looked pleased with their chore.

Stacks of West Berlin maps were available, helpful guides for East Berliners because the official East German maps showed only a blank space within the confines of the Wall.

"Why should I stay here?" He was puzzled by the idea that he might choose to stay on the West side. "I have a flat, and I'm a student. I have all I need also in our country. If I have the possibility of going to Western countries, that's enough for me." He smiled and laughed, "It's good to know that we can go wherever we want."

In those first three days, Kromphardt traveled through the Wall four times. "My first impression was many things are the same in East and West. It's normal to live here, and it's also normal to live in our country. People are very nice and that's very good."

But more than two hundred thousand East Germans decided to stay in the West. Some emigrated by foot, lugging suitcases through the border crossings. I watched at Friedrichstrasse as the guards processed the line-up as fast as possible, barely looking at travel documents.

The crowd was subdued, the travelers with luggage looking anxious as they passed by an old neon sign advertising an East German insurance company. *"Kasko,"* reminded the sign in typography from the thirties, *"bevor es zu spät ist."* "Kasko, before it's too late."

★ ★ ★

In those first heady days after the Wall opened, I spent time in the long lines in front of West Berlin banks. The East Germans were up at dawn, waiting patiently in the freezing November cold for the banks to open and dish out their free one hundred welcome deutsche marks.

Every East German had always been eligible for this spending money once a year, but until the Wall opened, only a few could get out of their side of Germany to collect the hard currency. Now the streets were jammed with these new tourists collecting the cash. In just a few days, while visas were still being issued for German-German border crossings and records were kept and correlated, six million East Germans crossed West. That's one third of the population.

They wandered around, or stood in the money lines, in shock, their eyes wide at the bombardment of their senses: flashy signs, jammed traffic, and the out-of-character warm welcome they were receiving from their Western cousins. They shuffled a little self-consciously waiting for the money, telling me they were happy for the opportunity to get some spending cash. Their own marks were virtually worthless on the West side of the Wall.

The Easterners were still a novelty item for the West Berliners. Shops and theaters offered big discounts if you flashed an East German identity card. The chilly Easterners lined up for the free money were looked at with a smile; still a few months off were the irritated and condescending scowls. With their money in hand, most of the newcomers headed for bananas, pineapples, oranges, and stereos. I asked one fellow who was buying fruit, "Is it really such a treat? Do you really not have bananas and oranges and pineapples?"

"Oh, we do," he told me, "one each at Christmas."

The wide-eyed visitors window-shopped endlessly, staring in stunned amazement at the variety and opulence available in rich West Berlin, at things we in the West take for granted: high-quality consumer goods, frivolous stuff, or just the fresh fruit.

The money was free. There was more. On the Gleineka Bridge between West Berlin and Potsdam, crowds surged West. This is the spy bridge, where the East and West swapped agents. Right after the Wall opened, it became a carnival.

Easterners were met at the border by Westerners passing out roses. Camel and Marlboro stationed cigarette giveaway crews right on the border. Huge Coke trucks were parked on the West side. Buses inched their way through the jam of cars and people, carrying more visitors into West Berlin. Drivers opened the bus doors, and the Coke gangs threw six-packs into the buses by the armful.

The Easterners laughed. They looked dizzy. This was the West. This was capitalism. Free flowers, cigarettes, and soda. Free money.

★ ★ ★

Up in one of the abandoned guard towers along the divide between East and West Berlin was an ideal vantage point for considering the new Germany. I climbed up into one a few months after that night the Wall opened. It was just down the street from Checkpoint Charlie but far from the beaten tourist track.

The neighborhood is mostly apartment buildings. A first wall that kept the neighbors from seeing the no-man's-land between it and the main wall was already wreckage when I climbed into the tower.

It was a chilling place to think about how quickly and radically life changed in Germany. The tower had been ransacked by the crowds that converged on the Wall in November. When I climbed up it was just a concrete shell; remnants of telephone connections were all that was left inside. Windows were shattered; so were the lens and bulb of the searchlight that had been used to pinpoint escapees just months before.

From the tower I looked out over the contradictions and schizophrenia that gripped Germany.

I looked at the no-man's-land that still separated East and West Berlin, and at the still present Wall. Border guards shooed away the curious from this strip. Passports and visas were still required to pass through the Wall, a restriction that couldn't end until the two Germanys united and the status of Berlin was determined.

It was a complex situation. West Berlin was never officially a part of West Germany, but an occupied city — occupied by the United States, France, and Great Britain. Final authority rested with the Allies. On the East side, the Soviet Union had turned over its authority to East Germany, but never gave up its rights as an occupational force. This allowed Soviet inspectors and soldiers to travel to the West side, just as the Allies could go over to the East side. It was an arrangement that benefited both: a window on the Soviets for the West, a chance to watch the Allies up close for the Soviets.

This complex establishment was what the "two plus four" meetings between the old World War II Allies and the two Germanys was set up to sort out. The details were figured out before Berlin reunited, but the changes happened so fast, and the superpowers were caught so off guard, that the Germans dictated most of the terms of their unification.

Interaction was already well underway in Berlin even before the Wall opened; the two sides were cooperating. The pace of the city coming back together accelerated remarkably after November. Travelers from the West to the East were no longer subjected to bizarre searches in those locked holding rooms for forbidden goods, like the latest edition of USA Today. Instead the border crossing became a simple formality. On the East side, even before the elections in March 1990, the West Germans installed public telephones hooked up directly to their phone system. That ended the ridiculous waits and the scratchy lines of just a few months before for calls back and forth across the line in Berlin.

The wires connecting up the public surveillance video cameras bolted to East Berlin lampposts were ripped apart. Police were busy directing traffic, not stopping people whimsically and checking papers. They no longer sat in their sidewalk boxes, peering out with binoculars through a slit of window so they could spy without being spied upon.

Campaign posters and random graffiti covered walls that had been previously kept absolutely clean of all but official messages.

Traffic filled the wide boulevards, roads that had been so empty just a few months before. Many of the license plates were West German; the rich-looking drivers of big Mercedes raced around looking for business opportunities.

Private street vendors set up impromptu shops—from card tables on the sidewalks and car trunks—selling formerly forbidden West German newspapers, fruits and vegetables, whatever people would buy.

Some merchants operated with two cash registers. One kept track of the sales that they were making in West German marks, the other, the less valuable East German marks.

Conversations were animated, politics the dominant theme.

Any of these activities—from cutting the camera wires to talking politics—could have meant jail just months before.

Life was radically different on the West side too. Traffic—
always grim in West Berlin—became intolerable as soon as the
Wall opened, and it only got worse as the months passed. And
worse than the grid lock was the smell imported from the East.
Taking full advantage of the new freedom to travel, Easterners
crossed the border daily by the thousands in their stinking, two-
cycle, smoking cars.

Downtown, the sidewalks were jammed to overflowing with
the influx of Easterners. They filled grocery stores looking for
items still hard to come by in the East. Boom boxes and all sorts
of electronic goodies were big sellers.

Immediately after the Wall opened, the Easterners were
warmly greeted as long-lost relatives. The Westerners were
giddy with delight, offering everything in sight to their long-
deprived cousins.

In just a few months that gave way to growing prejudice. The
new crowding was soon deplored. The shabby dress and naive
window-shopping of the East Germans were derided by the
sophisticated West Berliners.

Shopkeepers started complaining about shoplifting—pinpointing Easterners and saying the mentality of many of those
coming over for a look at the West side was negative. The
shopkeepers claimed that many Easterners carried through the
Wall with them an attitude that everyone on the West side is so
wealthy, it is okay to steal.

It was against this backdrop that the Germanys rushed toward
unification, a goal so many Germans had sought for so long and
then suddenly were forced to deal with as the reality of actually
getting together loomed closer and closer.

The list of unanswered questions was long, but as the first free
East German elections neared, a few problems towered over the
rest. East Germans feared that being part of the West meant
losing their state-provided social security as well as whatever
other positive elements existed in the separate German society
they had carved out of the war ruins for the last forty years.
Chancellor Helmut Kohl's party won the election in the East by
promising that the social security would not be lost, that the

East mark would even be exchanged one to one for the powerful West mark. But exactly how those goals would be accomplished was never made clear.

So West Germans worried that they'd be stuck with the bills, losing some of their wealth supporting their newfound compatriots.

It wasn't just a concern for the Germans, this ending of the division between the two Deutschlands. The rest of the world viewed a united Germany with concern and fear. Memories of World War II and the atrocities committed by the Nazis and the Germans created a public relations damage control job once the Wall opened.

The German question was no longer moot. The Allies were forced to face the consequences of their long and loud—but hollow—support for German unification. The West had misjudged the Soviet Union, which was, contrary to almost all political forecasters, finally giving up its European satellites. The division in Europe that had enabled the West to dodge the German question was disappearing. Gorbachev changed everything when he told the world that Eastern Europe was free to decide its own destiny, that the Brezhnev Doctrine was dead and Soviet troops would not be used to maintain the Soviet Empire in Eastern Europe.

German public relations experts suddenly found themselves needing to assuage world concern about a united Fatherland, and it was a job only made more difficult by Chancellor Kohl. Just as the world was getting ready to accept unification, he began to talk ambiguously about the future Polish-German border. Combined with crowds of East Germans screaming in unison *"Wir sind ein Volk!"* Kohl made the world nervous.

Looking down at East Berlin from the abandoned guard tower, I found myself feeling a certain nostalgia for the disappearing separate country of East Germany.

Of course, no one can miss the human rights violations, the perversion of shooting citizens who just want to travel, or the denial of an education to children of political opponents. But, at least for myself—an outsider visiting with the luxury of an exit visa — on my many trips into the East over the last decade, I had found, in the midst of the oppression and the ruined economy, some unique rays of light.

There was an appealing and romantic quiet on the East side, so unlike noisy West Berlin. I remember walking downtown one foggy night when my friend Markos made me stop and listen. From a couple of blocks away we could hear the scrape of a streetcar rounding a corner. The only other sounds were footsteps and the distant murmur of conversation.

The lack of flashy advertising was calming, too. A walk down the main streets was greeted with only a few subdued neon glows. In the smaller towns and out in East Berlin's suburbs, a visit was like time travel. In the cities little had changed since the 1930s. In the country, it often looked like the last century.

All that is changing fast. McDonald's plans to open restaurants all over the East. In a few years whatever separate identity East Germany forged those last forty years will be merely a historical footnote.

But the writer Philip Roth makes a convincing case for dismissing any lingering sentimentality about the old Eastern Europe in an interview in the *Paris Review*:

When I was first in Czechoslovakia it occurred to me that I work in a society where as a writer everything goes and nothing matters, while for the Czech writers I met in Prague, nothing goes and everything matters. This isn't to say I wished to change places. I didn't envy them their persecution and the way in which it heightens their social importance. Sometimes one or two writers with colossal brute strength do manage, miraculously, to survive and, taking the system as their subject, to make art of a very high order out of their persecution. But most of them who remain sealed up inside totalitarian states are, as writers, destroyed by the system. That system doesn't make masterpieces; it makes coronaries, ulcers, and asthma, it makes alcoholics, it makes depressives, it makes bitterness and desperation and insanity. The writers are intellectually disfigured, spiritually demoralized, physically sickened, and culturally bored. Frequently they are silenced completely. Nine-tenths of the best of them will never do their best work just because of the system. The writers nourished by this system are the party hacks. When such a system prevails for two or three generations, relentlessly grinding away at a community of writers for twenty, thirty, or forty years, the obsessions become fixed, the language grows stale, the readership slowly dies out from starvation, and the existence of a national literature of originality, variety, vibrancy (which is very different from the brute survival of a single powerful voice) is very nearly impossible. A literature that has the misfortune of remaining isolated underground for too long will inevitably become provincial, backwards, even naive, despite the fund of dark experience that may inspire it. By contrast, our work here hasn't been deprived of authenticity because as writers we haven't been stomped on by a totalitarian government.

Philip Roth's assessment of the effect of totalitarian government on writers holds true for the rest of the population, too. Only those who made their livings on the backs of their neighbors could truly miss the old days.

* * *

Should the rest of the world be concerned about a united Germany? Is there something inherently askew in the German character that explains the misery that nation and its leaders have caused the world this century?

One strong image of the Germans who just follow orders are the punkers in Berlin. They look like the picture of anarchy. They walk with a swagger to match James Dean's and wear tough-guy leather jackets with mean-looking studs sticking out all over. Their noses and ears are speared with a variety of antagonizing emblems. Their Technicolor hair stands on end in foot-high spikes, or their angry heads are shaved bald. When these symbols of rebellion saunter down the sidewalks of Berlin they look tough.

They look tough, that is, until they get to an intersection with a red light. Then, like most good Germans everywhere, they stand at the corner waiting for the Walk, Don't Walk light to turn green. They wait for that green light whether or not there is a car anywhere in sight.

Although this may be good news for traffic planners and a fine example for any little kids at the same street corners, it brings up some worrisome questions. If the meanest-looking, most contrary acts in town can't bring their punk selves to walk against the light, how healthy is individuality in Germany today?

Another case study: We're at a bowling alley in Berlin with our ten-year-old son, Michael. While we're playing, the automatic pin-setting machine makes a mistake and creates an opportunity for him to roll the ball at the pins an extra time during one of his turns. The machine forgot to clear the pins after his second shot.

As Michael is about to take this extra, free opportunity provided by faulty machinery, the good German playing in the adjacent alley walks over to our control panel. He smiles and pushes the reset button. Michael was not following orders. The German was enforcing the system. Would that scene have occurred in an American bowling alley?

Of course, there are exceptions to these stereotypes. Many Germans born after 1945 work hard to reject the negative characteristics that led to the horrors of the Nazi time. But there seems to be some reality to the idea that common characteristics exist in many Germans. Perhaps it is unwarranted prejudice to label Germans with negative national attributes, but the tendency to do just that seems to linger nonetheless. The worrisome combination that shows up over and over again in too many Germans is a lack of individuality and an easy acceptance of state-imposed authority.

One really offensive example of the gross differences in American and German official life is the *Anmeldung* law. All Germans must register with the police. They must inform the police where they live. If they move, they must — within just a week — inform the police of their new address.

That such a law exists is not what is confounding. The world is full of countries where the government keeps tight control on the citizenry. What's difficult to swallow is the blind acceptance most Germans show toward the registration requirement.

When I moved to Berlin, I asked friends and colleagues how to avoid the registration process. It offended me in principle. No one knew how to beat the system. Everyone complied. The registration papers are required for everything from getting gas and lights hooked up to securing a library card. It is part of society.

One German-language teacher of mine was irritated that so many Americans found the practice an invasion of privacy.

"It's a service," he insisted. "Suppose a friend of yours moves, or you lose his address. All you need to do is go to the police and you can find him again!"

Germans don't seem to understand that it is nobody's business where you live, particularly not the state and the police. If some people consider some sort of locator service valuable, they can form an organization and choose to register themselves.

That Germans consider it appropriate to register themselves with the government, especially in light of their recent Nazi history, is particularly disturbing. It is made only more disturbing when you check out the form used to keep track of people. Question 12 requires you write down your religion. There are only two correct alternatives: Protestant or Roman Catholic.

No big deal, say Germans, the question is there because the state provides tax money for the churches and needs to know how to disburse it to the two major religions in Germany. But if you are not Catholic or Protestant, or do not want your tax money to go to those churches, you must get a note from a preacher testifying to the tax collector that you do not attend one of the official churches.

In my Berlin neighborhood, die Meldestellen, the place to be registered was a huge police building. Gray walls and crowds greet the good citizen, along with a long wait. Take a number, instructs the sign. A board covers one wall, indicating how many customers are waiting and which interview room to go to once the number is finally called. Again, what's amazing is that so many Germans dutifully wait.[2]

---

[2]For more of the official and fatuous logic behind the Anmeldung law, consult the leaflet "Die Meldestellen," available from the Senator für Inneres Berlin, Fehrbeliner Platz 2, 1000 Berlin 31, Germany.

Tap another car's bumper while you're parking, and you'll immediately attract a crowd of Germans checking for damage. Smile and say hello to a stranger on the street, and you're suspicious. "I'm only here for the money," a Syrian falafel-maker told me in Berlin. "These people are *trochen und geschlossen*." Dry and closed.

Consider my friend Dagmar. I've known this artist for almost ten years. I've watched while she tried to get out of East Germany. I've visited her in her shabby little apartment in Dresden, looked at her trauma-filled gray paintings of women in distress.

She told me of reading a smuggled copy of *On the Road* when she was just twenty-one and how it changed her life. She decided then that she couldn't accept the Party line of the East German government. Finally, she married an American, an ex-GI, and after still another year of waiting, for a total of ten long years, her application for an exit visa was approved.

After the Wall opened, the letters that came from Dagmar expressed worry that the changes in the East allowed the old power structure to remain. "I saw a lot of SED [the German acronym for the old ruling Communist Party] friends of my mother at her birthday again," she wrote, "and now, after the revolution or whatever it was, after the end of the complete disaster, I saw the lying faces, a little bit more pale and a little bit more fat, but with the feeling that they still know the truth, but the truth sounds now completely different. The whole folk is demoralized, helpless, without fantasy."

She wasn't alone in her concern.

The Thatcher government called a cabinet-level meeting to discuss concern in the British government about German unification. The meeting started, according to the official minutes, with a listing of German "characteristics which you could identify from the past and expect to find in the future." Included were "angst, aggressiveness, assertiveness, bullying, egotism, inferiority complex, sentimentality."

★   ★   ★

When Dagmar visited us in America she decided to trade her bulky plastic glasses for a pair of contact lenses. She made an appointment at an eyewear outlet. Stuck in traffic on the way to the place, she started getting fidgety as ten o'clock rolled around. She wanted to hop out of the car and not wait to find a parking place.

It did no good to explain to her that the ten o'clock appointment was unimportant, that it was okay to just drop in anytime and order the contacts.

She kept looking at her watch, this avant-garde artist and refugee from totalitarianism. "You have to understand," she told my wife Sheila, "I am German."

★   ★   ★

But the world is betting that despite some irritating national characteristics, Germany is no longer a military threat. Perhaps its economic successes make military aggression unnecessary.

"Germany will be either a world power," Hitler wrote in *Mein Kampf*, "or will not be at all." It didn't happen his way, but it happened.

Chapter Four

THIRTY MILES TO POLAND

"These regions represent eight hundred years of German history, and they are an indispensable part of the German identity."
—Hartmut Koschyk, general secretary of the League of Expellees, discussing Polish territory just east of the Oder and Neisse rivers

THERE WAS A challenging, demanding look in the Polish man's eyes. We had just met at a party in a new apartment block on the outskirts of Poznan. He started quizzing me:

"What do you think of Poland? What do you think of Polish people? How do you think we live?"

I answered him cautiously, saying it wasn't my first trip to Poland, that I considered the country and the people normal, like countries and people everywhere.

"You aren't surprised by the color TV, by the VCR?"

I said no. I wasn't surprised. I'd been in the same apartment on my last trip to Poland a year before, and the always on and blasting TV had been an irritant then, too, but not a surprise.

He grabbed my hand and shook it hard up and down.

"I like you," he said, smiling. "Thank you for not thinking Poland is some wild and weird place. I'm glad you're not surprised that this is a normal apartment."

I soon liked Pawel Andrysiak, too. But he's wrong: Poland is a wild and weird place.

★　★　★

My first contact with Poland came just after Solidarity started organizing in 1980. I showed up at the Polish embassy in Vienna to get a visa. I spread my impressive NBC News credentials out in front of the visa officer and announced that NBC was sending me to report developments occurring in Poland.

The Polish embassy in Vienna is in an old villa, at that time sparsely furnished with just enough practical furniture like desks and chairs. We were sitting in a huge room with what once were ornate walls and ceilings. But it was now painted drab and just about empty. The officer's voice quietly echoed through the hollow room as he told me his government felt that enough foreign reporters were covering the story and that no more visas for reporters were being issued.

"Don't you have another profession?" he then asked.

"No, I'm a news reporter." I missed his point.

Apparently he wanted me to get into his country, because he continued.

"But don't you do something else, too?"

I was stupidly insistent, "No, I'm a news reporter."

"I know that." He patiently worked with me. "But don't you do some other work, perhaps you also do some teaching. We have another embassy in Budapest."

He could see that he wasn't getting through.

"You can apply again for a tourist visa in Budapest."

Finally I understood, and a couple of days later, as a high school history teacher from California, I was headed for Ferihegy Airport in Budapest with my Polish visa stamped in my passport.

* * *

Most of Eastern Europe's 1989 revolutionaries appreciate Gorbachev for his contribution to their success. They know that no matter how spirited and brave, creative and frustrated they were as they overthrew their dictators, they succeeded so quickly because of Gorbachev's decision not to interfere. But though they acknowledge Gorbachev, many Eastern Europeans understand that the groundwork done against the Communist regime in Poland helped the anti-Communist cause all across the Eastern bloc.

Postwar opposition to Soviet domination of Poland can be traced to Poznan and 1956. Workers protested difficult living conditions; their demonstrations were put down, leaving scores dead and more arrested. But then, when Polish Communist Party leaders refused to follow orders from Moscow about how to govern following the uprising, Khrushchev threatened to impose his will on the Poles with Soviet troops. The Poles matched his threats with a threat to fight back.

The Soviets did not invade, and the first postwar housecleaning of Soviet influence started in Poland. Soviet operatives were dispatched home, and restrictions on personal liberties were eased. But over the next generation, the Polish Communists maintained control, with periodic crackdowns whenever Poles pushed so hard for freedoms that the Party felt its authority was in jeopardy.

In 1968, international student revolts made their way to Poland and were crushed. In 1970, shipyard workers at Gdansk led strikes against higher food prices. These demonstrations, too, were stopped by force. Strikers at the Lenin Shipyard were killed as the strike was broken.

Economic problems — specifically food shortages and rising food prices — triggered strikes again in 1980, again starting at the Lenin Shipyard. This time the Poles had the benefit of the charismatic strike leader Lech Walesa and a national political alternative to the Communists: the Solidarity trade union. Initially the government attempted to work with Solidarity. But as the union's power grew and threatened Communist rule, the Party responded by imposing martial law and outlawing Solidarity at the end of 1981.

General Wojciech Jaruzelski, looking like a caricature of a bad guy with his medal-strewn officer's uniform, stiff back, and dark glasses, insisted the alternative to Polish martial law was a Soviet invasion. Walesa was sent to jail and won the Nobel Peace Prize. Solidarity hung together, underground. Poland became outwardly calm again.

By the late 1980s, martial law had been lifted, Solidarity was again legal, and the economy was still a mess, and Jaruzelski presided over the demise of the Communist government. Gorbachev was in charge in the Soviet Union, and Soviet troops were no longer a threat. The general negotiated with the opposition to hold free elections, elections that by the end of 1990 ousted the Communists from power and elevated Welesa to the presidency.

Just before Jaruzelski yielded the Polish presidency to Welesa—the opponent he had sent to prison—the general spoke to the nation on TV, answering complaints about his policies. He insisted that any Polish misery resulting from his rule "hurts me like a thorn in my flesh. As a soldier," he tried to explain, "I know that the commander is responsible for every man and everything. The words 'I apologize' may sound banal. But I cannot find any other words."

★ ★ ★

Gdansk is a gritty seaport. One of the early demands of the 1980 shipyard strikers was that the government build a memorial to their comrades who died during the 1970 strike. The soaring three crosses of the monument tower on the horizon at the entrance to the shipyard, a reminder that the sudden changes of the late eighties were long in coming. On the west side of the city, apartment houses march toward the countryside, huge blocks of anonymity.

We stayed at the Grand Hotel in the adjacent resort city Sopot. The Grand is a sprawling hunk of a building right on the beach. It is crumbling from deferred maintenance. One clever example was the bathtub of our room. Somewhere along the line, the faucet and taps needed some repair, and clearly the tile work had been chipped away to allow the plumber access to the pipes. Instead of trying to patch up the tiling, an old ornate serving platter had been used to cover the gaps left in the wall over the tub. Touches like the flowery platter glued to the wall gave the Grand a friendly human warmth. The hotel's grandeur is not completely faded; the dining room is still elegant, the food fresh and fancy.

"Herr Laufer! Herr Laufer!" The smiling Polish woman followed me out the door of the official Polish government travel agency, Orbusz, after I made reservations for the Grand. We were in Berlin, and she spoke in heavily accented German, giving the language an appealing singsong sound. "Herr

Laufer!" Once she had my attention she dropped her voice to conspiratorial tones, much as the visa officer had in Vienna, and she advised, "Offer to pay in deutsche marks. It will cost very little."

So we asked the waiter if he minded marks instead of zlotys, and he became much more interested in us; he wanted the convertible money. Three full meals with beer and wine cost us five marks, less than three dollars at the time. During this period of transition for the economy, the bargains for those of us spending Western hard currency were ridiculous. But as cheap as the meal was for us, it was inaccessible to most Poles. They were struggling just to provide the basics for themselves, their wages trailing far behind increasing prices.

Swans played on the Sopot beach. On the main street, shady-looking characters in cheap leather jackets hung out around the bank. They were black-market money changers. By this time, changing money on the street was no longer illegal, but these guys still acted as if they were hiding something from someone. They met their customers with a knowing glance at the bank and then walked slowly down side streets making calculations, negotiating. Money was exchanged with quick movements, and then the customer and the money changer quickly split. Perhaps it was just custom, after so many years of hiding from the law. Maybe there was some latent (understandable) fear that the rules and laws could change again, even retroactively, and it was safer not to be blatant. The exercise was repeated all day long at the bank and added an overtone of mystery to the off-season resort.

★ ★ ★

Poznan is near the Oder-Neisse Line, on the other side of Poland from Sopot and Gdansk. Over the last eight hundred years it has been alternately Germany and Poland. When Stalin carved a hunk out of the eastern side of Poland for the Soviet Union after the war, Poland was compensated with acreage from Hitler's Reich that now makes up Poland's western lands.

One result of the historically slippery border is that Poles hate Germans and Germans hate Poles. Or perhaps the slippery border is the result of the hate and distrust between Poles and Germans. Now that both nations are rid of their Communist governments, there is no longer any reason to maintain a facade of socialist brotherhood.

Europeans behind the rising Iron Curtain do hate one another in a manner difficult for an American to understand. Montanans tell disparaging jokes about people from North Dakota. Old-time Nevadans are irritated about the influx of new settlers from California. Southerners still react negatively to Yankees. But such American regional conflict is superficial and rarely extends to personal rejection of individuals.

By contrast, in Eastern Europe, prejudice is deep and complete. The long years of Stalinist rule gave the Eastern Europeans a common enemy: their own governments. Nationalist chauvinism was kept to a minimum, officially. "They hate Poles," Pawel, the fellow at the party in Poznan who shook my hand so happily, says of the Germans. "I'm a Pole. I must say, I hate them."

Poznan is slowly shaking off its Communist gray veneer. But the rusting trams still rattle along the tracks; they don't swoosh along like their West European counterparts. Display signs are still more often restrained neon tubes than brightly lit plastic. Exceptions to the peeling paint and cracked plaster are rare, like the new British-owned casino. Even the French chain Novotel manages to create the almost comfortable worn and dingy feel that identifies Eastern Europe today.

At first this state of decay is disconcerting to most Western visitors. But it can become friendly, especially compared with the brash and removed glitz of West Germany. Poznan is being lived in; it's being used.

We left West Berlin after dinner, for Poland. I was with Grzegorz and Mariosz. It was late winter in 1990, after the Berlin Wall had fallen, but before the East German elections. The Communist bureaucracy was still trying to hang on, many of the old rules were still in place. The two of them are Polish auto mechanics, working for hard currency, for deutsche marks, in West Berlin and commuting home to Poznan every weekend. I was going along to spend the weekend and see what life is like for them there, where they live like royalty because of their West money.

We got into Grzegorz's long new Mercedes and slipped out onto the autobahn. The first border stop comes in just a few miles, leaving West Berlin and heading into East Germany.

All this has changed now, with the unification of Germany. But back when the borders between East and West Germany and between West Berlin and East Germany were fortified international frontiers, there were only two crossings where foreigners were allowed by the East Germans to leave West Berlin and head out of Germany.

A direct line from Berlin to the Polish border is just about thirty miles. The drive for Grzegorz, Mariosz, and me takes about twice that. The Iron Curtain rose fast, but despite the revolution in East Germany, five months later when we took our trip together, the crazy travel restrictions imposed around the old German capital remained. From the Allied sector of Berlin, we must drive west. Poland is east.

YOU ARE LEAVING THE AMERICAN SECTOR. The sign is huge, translated into German, French, and Russian. There's no mistaking that you're about to drive across a radical cultural and political barrier. A gas station offers a last chance to fill up with Western gas. Plenty of regular travelers across East Germany insist that even though the gas is cheaper in East Germany, it's bad for cars, perhaps watered down. The border gas station is the last chance to pay for gas with a credit card, the last chance — except for a few special Communist government stores — to buy rich West German chocolates and ice-cream and dirty West German girlie magazines and to use relatively clean West German toilets. Hitchhikers line the few hundred feet between the gas station and the West German border station, waving destination signs.

The barrier is clear. After the American sector line, there is no fooling around. No hitchhikers, no commercial stuff like gas stations with flashy signs advertising newspapers and candies. It's all serious government business: barricades, fences, stern speed limits, and a huge Soviet tank mounted on a concrete pedestal.

At first sight, the border fortifications are intimidating, the guards watching without a hint of a smile, machine guns ready, the miles of fencing, the cleared no-man's-land between fences. After several trips back and forth, the militarized border no longer generates fear. That emotion is replaced with disgust for the stupidity of a system that turned an entire country into a prison camp.

As usual, the crossing out of Berlin is no problem for us that night. The Allies and the West German border guards are not interested in who is leaving, especially since Grzegorz's Mercedes is equipped with West Berlin license plates.

It's all slightly more complicated as we make our way the few hundred meters up to the East German checkpoint. The border here changed remarkably in the few months following the opening of the Berlin Wall. The paranoia has diminished to almost nil. The automatic devices designed to shoot steel barriers across the highway at the flick of a switch if the guards decide they don't want you to enter or leave the DDR are permanently open and already show signs of having been damaged by the jackhammers and blowtorches of road crews assigned to remove them. Up at the main border building, the conveyor belts are off, the first checkpoint is shut down, and we drive up to what is almost a normal international border scene: one check for passports and another by customs agents.

During the height of the paranoid Honecker regime in East Germany, passports were checked once and then sent on the conveyor belt up to a second checkpoint to make sure border guards couldn't be bribed. Two separate checks of travel papers took place, by two separate guards in two separate guard huts.

Grzegorz and Mariosz have permanent resident status in Berlin, so they are allowed to transit East Germany freely. I have an East German multiple entry visa that allows me to travel freely all over East Germany. But that does not entitle me to transit the country freely. I must buy a five-mark visa (these are West marks that the East German government charges, one

more device to provide the country with needed hard currency)
to allow me to use the transit road.

We get past the border, and Grzegorz takes a radar detector
out of the glove compartment, plugs it into the cigarette lighter,
and hooks the device to the visor. He leans back in his seat and
lights the first of his chain-smoked cigarettes for the trip ahead.
He slips what will turn out to be an endless Barry White cassette
into the tape player, and we head out toward the Berliner Ring
to make our way back onto the autobahn toward Poland.

We talk about politics ("Lech Walesa is getting fat"), wives,
cars, making money. Barry White drones in the background
about his women.

After a couple of hours clattering along the bad pavement, we
get to Frankfurt an der Oder, the main crossing point into
Poland. And the cars are backed up—backed way up. This is
where, a year before, I had met Grzegorz. I had been stuck
behind him in the border traffic jam, I noticed his West German license plates, and got out to chat.

"Four-hour wait," he had told me then. I laughed back at him
and said it was impossible we would be stuck four hours, since it
was only a couple of thousand meters up to the border.

"Four-hour wait," he had assured me. We spent the time
talking. I made coffee on the stove in my camper; he pulled
beers out of his trunk.

There are alternatives to waiting patiently in line. Every few
minutes a car would stubbornly edge into the lane of oncoming
traffic and start passing our stopped cars. It would squeeze
against the stopped cars to dodge cars and trucks coming out of
Poland on the two-lane strip and then continue to make its way
toward the border. The routine was simple for busting the line,
Grzegorz told me:

"A twenty-mark—West mark—bill folded into the passport
for the guard at the first checkpoint."

But the system doesn't always work. I was annoyed watching
the cheats. I shook my fist at one car and yelled, and that
seemed to motivate the Poles a few cars back. As the next
cheater approached, a bunch of bored and irritated men got out

in the road and blocked the old gray Russian sedan. The driver tried to edge on through, but the crowd beat their fists on his car and yelled and intimidated him into turning around.

"One time," Grzegorz told me as the now-inspired crowd prepared to stop the next intruder, "I watched a bunch of guys stop and pick up a car that was passing and throw it into the ditch."

By the time our four hours were up, he helped me get through the complicated paperwork at the border and insisted that we follow him to his house and meet his wife.

The four-hour wait is only because of inefficiency and lack of concern. The border guards are simply in no hurry. Moving people and commerce quickly and smoothly is a foreign concept to them.

There are two sets of guards. First come the passport check guards, both East German and Polish. As long as all papers are in order, there really is nothing for these guards to do except stamp the visas and passports. And that is all they do. But they do it remarkably slowly. Even physically the border is set up to slow progress. You must stop your car at the border and get out and walk up to the windows where the guards do their slow paperwork inspections.

Next come the customs guards, again East German and Polish. They, too, do no real checking of baggage or car trunks. They just slowly pore over meaningless forms, like lists of how much money you're carrying. No one cares what you're really carrying, just that you fill out the form more or less correctly.

Once the four-hour wait is passed, and you're finally heading into Poland, it's quite easy to lose track of one little scrap of paper that gets added to your stack of documents somewhere along the way, but it's a crucial scrap. That's the scrap that's collected by the guard who darts out of the dark from a tiny hut at the end of the border complex. Without it, you go back and try to convince the guards at the other end to give you another.

It was close to midnight when we barged into the apartment unannounced. We couldn't call ahead, Grzegorz had been waiting years for a telephone. But his wife was unruffled seeing all of us at the door. She rubbed her eyes and laughed, "He does this all the time!"

Now, a year later, Grzegorz eyeballed the line of cars at the border and again predicted, "Four hours."

He swung the car around, consulted in Polish with Mariosz, and told me, "We're going south to another crossing; it will be quicker to go out of the way than to wait here."

We headed south toward Cobush, past mile after mile of factories lining the road, through little villages, and finally to the border crossing at Eisenhüttenstadt. There were only a few cars ahead of us. But attracted by our Berlin license plates, a guard came up to the car and checked our papers.

The two of them were fine, Poles in transit to Poland. But the East German guard insisted that I could not cross at this point. The problem was that I am an American citizen with an American passport. By the perverse logic of the system still in effect, the Poles could transit into Poland because that is their home, even though they were traveling from West Berlin where they worked. But I was restricted to a very few border crossings earmarked for foreigners who were just crossing through East Germany. The fact that I was in possession of a valid visa for traveling all over the DDR did not impress the border guard.

"That is for traveling around the DDR, not for leaving the country. You can only leave through transit points," he told me.

We argued with him, explaining that we had already traveled far out of our way, that it was late at night.

He was unimpressed, and again, Grzegorz turned the car around as we headed still farther south to another border crossing, this one government approved for transiting Americans.

"This is why there will continue to be problems here." Grzegorz was resigned to the extra driving but irritated. The mentality of the guard was evidence for him of a kind of German thinking that wasn't going to go away just because the Wall was open and the two Germanys were on the road to unification.

The guard could have let us through. During this period of transition in East Germany, the rules were often being changed—even made up at the borders on the spur of the moment. Certainly there would have been no retribution against the guard if he had let us through.

Instead we drove on through the night and finally made it into Poland at Forst. Again, this was no quick check. It took about an hour to get through the border. The Iron Curtain is rising—but it is thick. The stupidity, unnecessary regulations, and paperwork that have bottled up culture and prosperity throughout the Eastern bloc since the war are not going away overnight.

The guards on both sides of the border labored over our papers before we finally made it into Poland. The ethnic and attitude differences were clear: the passport and the customs guards sit alongside one another in adjoining, but separate, offices. The Germans sit up straight, looking full of business. On the Polish side the mood is much more relaxed, uniforms rumpled and sloppy, ties loose. There's lots of chatter and joking around on the Polish side.

We made our way into the Baltona shop to see if there was anything good and cheap available. During this time of transition in Poland, the Baltona shop is a remnant of the old system. Despite the radical changes in the political and economic systems, much remains the same. The shop sells Western goods, inside Poland, for Western currency. The idea is that the government finds bargains on the world market and then uses these shops to undercut Western stores and draw hard currency from travelers: Communists playing capitalism. But the line was long, and we saw nothing that we couldn't get for just pennies more in West Berlin: Marlboros, Legos, coffee, and liquor.

So we headed on into the Polish night. On other trips, later, I would see this part of Poland in the daytime. It is farming land punctuated periodically with a crossroads village or a roadhouse. The landscape is not unlike northern Illinois and Indiana, where so many Poles settled in America.

We sped on, the needle on the gas gauge falling. We saw a gas station in the distance, and Grzegorz drove on past it and pulled up alongside some trees just out of sight. He hopped out and opened the trunk. It was a well-planned exercise. Mariosz jumped out too, grabbed a gas can out of the trunk, and headed off through the cold night toward the gas station, huddled against the wind.

"We cannot buy gas without coupons," Grzegorz explained to me, "because of the Berlin license plates."

The Berlin license plates give Grzegorz all sorts of advantages in Berlin—like not having to worry about his windows being smashed by marauding bands of Germans looking for Polish cars to trash. Once he gets home to Poland, it causes him a little grief to cruise around in the big Mercedes with the D for Deutschland sticker. First of all, the Poles think he's a German. But maybe more important, he can buy gas only with special coupons for foreigners. It's part of the mess of an economy that still exists in the East.

Mariosz was off in the distance. "They'll sell him gas," Grzegorz explained. "They'll think he's some poor Polish man that they must help."

But Mariosz came back without gas. The station was closed. Barry White lamented on as we slowed up to save fuel and kept on toward Poznan.

The exercise was repeated several more times—a slide past a gas station looking for life, then a stop a few hundred yards away. Up comes the trunk, and Mariosz runs off looking lonesome and in need. But every station was closed. In Eastern Europe, you can't determine that a business is closed just because the place is dark. Often the lights are off to save electricity, and a dark, deserted-looking store may well be open and full of customers.

Just as we got to Poznan, we ran out of gas. The car came to a stop with a thud up on the curb. We dribbled the gas can upside down, and a liter or two came out. We made it to the Poznan gas station, Mariosz had a few words with the gas station attendant, and we pulled the big Mercedes right up to the pumps.

Grzegorz winked, "Here in Poznan all is possible." They knew the attendant, they gave him some extra money, or both. Maybe they slipped him a little hard currency. I was too tired to check.

I woke up the next morning in Grzegorz and Lucynna's apartment. Polish Radio Three was blasting, "Oh, lonesome me . . ." Radio Three always plays British and American pop music. Lucynna listens for the English. She wants to learn "American English. I want to speak like an American. I've always had this dream to come to America." She keeps the TV on in the living room, the radio on in the dining room. She doesn't want to miss anything. She gets mad when someone turns one of them down. They're both on unless it's time to sleep.

The apartment is a new one in a block among other blocks of apartments. The two of them lived with his mother downtown until they were able to move in. Outside there's no landscaping, and there's nothing to indicate there ever will be any landscaping. Huge holes in the yard are filled with water from the last rains. The entryway is institutional gray; the tin mailboxes look shabby; there's no elevator.

But once inside, their apartment is middle-class palatial. In the living room, the TV is enormous, hooked up to cable and complete with a video player. We watched home videos of their last vacation to Turkey. The stereo is the latest stuff; the couch is sprawling. The red-and-white-tiled bathroom is spotless; there's a late-model washing machine alongside the bathtub. The kitchen is color-coordinated, with bright yellow coffeemaker, meat slicer, and all sorts of other efficient gadgets.

The two of them have found a way to play the best of both systems. Trading their hard Western currency in Poland gives them phenomenal buying power in zlotys. At the same time, they can take advantage of all that West Berlin has to offer, dragging home whatever latest toys and conveniences the West makes and sells.

★   ★   ★

We're in downtown Poznan. We've toured the main square and admired the old Dutch-influenced buildings that circle the city hall. The houses are faded, but well preserved. It's a visual relief that they don't shine with the super-restored gleam of old villages in West Germany. These Poznan relics are lived in, and used, and their roughness gives the neighborhood a more authentic appearance, as does the lack of ice-cream, postcard, and other tourist junk shops on the street.

"I don't like it; it looks like Istanbul," says Lucynna. We're a few blocks away from the old downtown and checking out the street vendors peddling stereos, clothes, toys, oranges. Just a few months before, such selling was illegal. Lucynna, dressed to the nines in her West Berlin outfit, her house full of West Berlin food and furniture, doesn't like seeing the streets of Poznan littered. She recognizes the double standard but remains annoyed with the street market as we chew on some salty cheese that we buy from a peasant woman down for a few days' selling from her home in the Tatra Mountains.

The switch to a free market economy isn't making life easier yet for most Poles. "Before," I keep hearing, "we had plenty of money and nothing to buy. Now there's everything available, but there's no money."

And, in fact, the prices on the street in the private ad hoc markets are quite incredible: A couple of dollars for a bag of oranges—about the same as I'd pay in California, but the average monthly salary is running at about sixty dollars in Poland. Sixty dollars. If jeans are thirty dollars and a bag of oranges two dollars, it just doesn't help much that subsidized rents keep apartments at around twelve dollars a month.

But for Grzegorz and Lucynna, the twelve dollars that they pay each month for their apartment is a real bargain. With his West Berlin mechanic's wages, Grzegorz can afford to bring West German goods to Poland and buy the new luxuries available at the Polish street markets. Not only does he earn enough money to support a decent standard of living in West Berlin, he changes his hard currency into zlotys on the black market when he's home in Poland. The difference in currency values is so extraordinary that whatever he buys with his zlotys is virtually free.

By the end of 1990, even with Poland and many of the other Eastern bloc countries moving as fast as they could away from Communism and toward capitalism, none of the East bloc currencies, except the Yugoslavian dinar, were convertible. Convertible currencies, or hard currencies, are money you can take from one country and exchange for the money of another

country. Because the centrally planned economies of the Eastern bloc were artificial economies, with prices subsidized and
wages fixed, the value of the currency did not equate to any
international economic reality. Outside the Eastern bloc, the
European Communist currencies were essentially without
value.

In order to buy something from a Western economy, those
stuck behind the Iron Curtain, whether governments or individuals, either needed access to hard Western currencies or bar-
tered with goods and services. The easiest route to hard
currency for most people was to sell their own money cheap on
the black market. By undercutting the high, unrealistic official
exchange rate, the black marketeers offered great bargains to
travelers with dollars and marks. In an effort to stem the black
market in money, many of the East bloc countries forced Western visitors to exchange enough money at the official rate to pay
for most of their needs during their stay, consequently reducing
the demand for black market money.

★ ★ ★

Pawel and Krzysztof came over to Grzegorz and Lucynna's
apartment with their wives for a few drinks. Pawel's an architect,
but he can't make decent money that way, so he's selling tile and
marble building supplies. Krzysztof can't practice his profession
either if he wants to make a reasonable wage. He's an engineer,
but for the last several years he's been running a couple of private
grocery stores. The two merchants are worried now that money
is getting tight. Business is slowing for luxuries like the Western
groceries that Krzysztof sells. He's branching out. Now that
private gun ownership is again legal, he's going into the weapons
trade.

Both are gregarious, in their thirties.

Pawel's the one who asks me, "What do you think of Poland?"

I respond slowly, not because the language is much of a
barrier—we're using both English and German—but because
it's clear that the question is some sort of setup.

"It's interesting to be here," I told him. "I like to see what's
going on in the rest of the world and meet people."

He was demanding: "You aren't surprised to find such a nice apartment, the TV, the stereo?"

I was slow again with my response; now that I knew his direction, I wanted to reinforce his satisfaction.

"No, why should I be surprised? It's a normal apartment. I've been to Poland before. What should I be surprised about?"

That's when he got up and jabbed his hand out, grabbing mine to shake and made his announcement to the room: "I like you because you don't think Poland is some weird, wild place. I like you because you think Poland is normal."

He smiled.

Later we played poker. Pawel dragged out a big plastic bag full of one-zloty coins. At that time ten thousand zlotys came to about a dollar. We used the zlotys as chips, the game degenerating as the players drank.

As the night progressed there was less and less English and German spoken, more of the Polish that I could not understand. Suddenly the three of them, Pawel, Krzysztof, and Grzegorz were laughing and laughing. The chuckles became uncontrollable giggles and then hysteria.

When they recovered, I got the translation.

At this point Pawel had accumulated most of the chips. He was still laughing.

"I've got a good hand," he told me, breaking up again, "but they've got no money left to bet." Exactly what they were experiencing in real life in Poland.

We talked about the united Germany. Pawel again was the most animated and insistent. "DDR people are something different after forty years of fascism. They hate Poles, and as a Pole, I must say, I hate them."

He wasn't worried about the equivocation by Kohl on the Polish-German border situation. He doesn't fear a military invasion by the united Germany; he worries about their economic strength. His concern is that the Germans, who are already cruising Poland looking around, will simply come back to this former German territory and buy what they want.

By the end of 1990, the unified Germany did finally sign a border treaty with the Poles, officially recognizing as permanent the Oder-Neisse Line as the border between the two countries. The German foreign minister, Hans-Dietrich Genscher, used the ceremony to try to mollify tensions. "We Germans," said Genscher, "are aware that the treaty reflects no new territory losses, but rather confirms what was long since lost in a criminal war and a criminal system."

Grzegorz, too, is irritated by the East Germans. When we were turned back at the border because we were at the crossing that was not legal for me to cross with a transit visa, he spoke of the situation as an example of why he sees nothing but trouble for a united Germany. He's convinced that it will take a long time for the two Germanys to work out their differences and act as one unit. The East Germans, he told me, especially the foot soldiers out in the sticks, don't know how to think independently. They only know how to follow rules.

He took a thick historical atlas off his bookshelf and leafed through it with me, showing the Polish border moving back and forth over the centuries. Sometimes the Polish nation controls land all the way to the Black Sea. Sometimes it's so tiny it's hard to find on the map.

He shrugs. He's already transcended the boundaries. He works around the politicians. He points to the always-on TV. A stereotypical newscaster is droning in Polish.

Grzegorz translates. The commentary is anti-Qaddafi. The reporter looks earnest.

"Just before the government changed, this same reporter announced programs praising Qaddafi," Grzegorz was disgusted. "Suddenly he showed up with the opposite point of view, and with no explanation of the change."

★   ★   ★

Solidarity provided the political focus for the Poles' fight against their Communist government. With virtually the entire Jewish population exterminated during the War, most Poles today are Catholics, and the church remained a vital element of Polish society all through the years of Communist domination. Active church support for Solidarity and the support for opposition to the government expressed by Pope John Paul II — the first Polish pope — gave actual and spiritual help to those working to change the system.

Polish Catholics flock to Czestochowa to pray to the painting of the Black Madonna. It was raining when we made our way from the muddy parking lot into the Jasna Gora Monastery complex to see the icon for ourselves. The legend is that the picture came from Jerusalem. It was slashed by invading Swedish Protestants, but then the Madonna intervened to help Polish soldiers defeat the invaders and keep Poland free. Now the remnants of that cut appear to the faithful pilgrims as tears.

The monastery is always jammed, absolutely filled to standing room only, with worshipers trying to catch a glimpse of the Madonna. She is kept in a church on the monastery grounds, and twice a day a silver curtain rolls up, exposing the picture for a few minutes. The walls of the church are covered with crutches and other reminders of the infirmities cured by the Madonna.

The silver curtain rises, trumpets sound, and the crowd sings. The experience is inspiring, if only because of the deep piety of the pilgrims.

In the face of this overwhelming Catholicism, and a rising throng of unemployed and underemployed, anti-Semitism became a serious component of the 1990 presidential election, despite the fact that the postwar Jewish population in Poland is just a token few thousand.

Lech Walesa was charged by his opponents during the election with fomenting the anti-Semitic mood by campaigning as a "hundred percent Pole, going back generations." Another statement used by Walesa that was interpreted as anti-Semitic code was his promise to "introduce a clear system of government; everyone will know who is who and where he comes from."

*   *   *

"Walesa is getting fat," Grzegorz complained. His enthusiasm for the changes in Poland was subdued. Pleased with lifted restrictions, he saw no cause for making the new leaders of the country into heroes, instead dismissing them with the rejection, "They're all the same criminals."

Grzegorz was not alone in deciding not to vote for the Solidarity hero. "Walesa is not educated as a leader," he said just before the election. "He's okay for a union, but not for a nation."

Walesa finally was elected, but by a much smaller margin than he expected. He was no longer the hero who led Poland peacefully out of Communism, but just another politician.

★   ★   ★

With desperate patience, hundreds of Poles lined up every day at the Aldi near the Zoo train station in West Berlin, waiting for the supermarket to open. They filled other Aldis around West Berlin, too. Aldi is a bare-bones discount store with changing stock. You can't be sure what you'll find, but you are guaranteed low prices. The decor is basic: cardboard cartons full of chocolate bars, cans of *würst*, and toilet paper; stacks of cases of beer; boxes of orange juice.

The poor Polish traders cleaned off the shelves, jammed their tiny Polski Fiats with cheap beer and cigarettes, and headed back to Poland to re-sell the stuff for a thin profit.

Rich West Berliners dodged the long lines, cursing their newly crowded streets — cursing the Poles for making shopping a pain, cursing the cleaned-out shelves in the markets. The Berliners didn't like the Poles littering their sidewalks with the long lines. The dingy dress and drawn, hungry faces of the Polish traders were irritating. The reminder of tough times annoyed the rich Berliners.

When the oppressive East bloc governments locked their citizens behind the borders, making travel abroad difficult if not impossible, West Berlin was held out as a beacon. "This is the good life!" screamed the West. "This is the life you can have if you get rid of your Communists!"

But the message was not intended for the poor Poles lined up in front of the Aldi. It was not an offer to share the wealth. It was just another battle in the cold war. It was part of the charade that the West felt comfortable perpetrating: led by America, the

West promoted knocking down the Berlin Wall, uniting Germany, getting rid of the Iron Curtain.

It was a safe policy. Up on the moral high road, the West felt secure in calling for these dramatic changes, convinced the Communists would never really bend. Communists had never given up any turf. The insecure Western policymakers believed their own propaganda. They had created such a monolithic enemy in Communism, it never occurred to them that such a powerful system might collapse. They seduced their poor cousins stuck behind the Iron Curtain with the offer of West Berlin and the great Western paradise in the lands of the other side of the Iron Curtain, not because they wanted the West crawling with refugees from Communism, but as a propaganda ploy.

West Berlin was wide open for Poles and other citizens of the Eastern bloc. All they had to do was get their own governments to allow them to travel west, and they were welcomed by West Berlin's open border. No visas were required. Of course, the number of travelers was minimal; few could obtain the necessary exit papers from their own countries. Even fewer could muster the hard Western currency needed to spend even a minimal amount of time in expensive West Berlin.

But as Eastern European Communist governments began to crack, the rules started changing fast. Berlin filled up with day-tripping Poles, lured by the opportunity to make a few black market deutsche marks. Vacant lots near the Wall turned into the Polish flea market.

Thousands of Poles made the trip West on weekends, selling family heirlooms, subsidized consumer products brought over from the Eastern bloc, handicrafts, homemade food — whatever they figured would bring in a few marks.

The first hint of official restrictions on the open invitation showed up on the autobahns into West Berlin, when the West German Zollpolizei established the separate lane for cars with East bloc license plates and began inspecting them for merchandise that looked intended for resale. Cars were turned back for violating commerce restrictions.

By the time the two Germanys had worked out unification details, no one was hiding prejudice. Berlin was no longer available to the wandering victim of Communism. All travelers from the Eastern bloc, even with the Iron Curtain rising, suddenly needed visas to cross the border into Germany.

The East bloc governments no longer restricted their citizens' travel plans, but the doors were still hard for Eastern Europeans to open. Now their Western neighbors had second thoughts about open-ended invitations. The official excuse for the new visa restrictions was the sprawling West Berlin flea market. The West Berlin government insisted visas were needed to control illicit trading.

The duplicity of the new requirements that forced Poles and other Eastern Europeans to obtain visas before coming to Germany didn't last long. Public pressure convinced the Germans the reduced traffic in Poles wasn't worth the bad worldwide publicity, and the border was opened again to incoming Poles. But the prejudice remained.

★   ★   ★

Lucynna and Grzegorz want to have a baby. She's going into the hospital for a few days of tests. She explains to me that she must bribe the doctor.

"We have free medical care here in Poland. That's what everybody says. Yes, it's free, but if I go to the doctor and say I want these tests, I'll be told that I must wait a year or two. There are no beds available in the hospital. Yes, it's free, but it's not available."

So she puts an envelope on the doctor's desk as they talk. The hospital bed is arranged for two days later.

I ask her how she knows how much money to put in the envelope. Lucynna and her friends discussed the bribing, and together came up with an amount they thought was right.

"She treats me well, so I guess it's enough."

She worries about her hospital stay. "Polish hospitals are so dirty."

Will she have a TV?

She smiles, "Oh, yes, I'll have a TV in the room." Pause. "I'll have a TV in the room because I'll bring one."

★   ★   ★

No matter how disgusted we are with the mess we see in Eastern Europe, we—as Americans, as people lucky enough to live where we are free, or relatively free, to do what we want to do—cannot even begin to judge the actions of people who lived under the oppression of the dictatorships there. We can hope that we would have responded by leaving, or fighting for change. But those of us who have never been tested by such conditions should not show too much impatience with scenes like little old ladies standing complaisantly in freezing lines outside markets even though there is room inside the relatively warm stores. That's just one example of the day-to-day oppression these women are forced to accept as part of their routines. They've been fed rules and terms of existence from overlords with guns and power to enforce their regulations. Those of us who have not had to face loss of professional opportunities, imprisonment, and death for opposing our governments are in a weak position to criticize the manner in which other people respond to such indignities.

Back in 1980, I watched those lines in Warsaw. It was deep winter. The days were short and cold. In front of the little shops, lines stretched—grandmothers huddled against the cold, weighed down with packages, the snow collecting on their threadbare coats. They waited to get into shops displaying lengths of shriveled sausages, gray hunks of meat.

Ten years later, I joined a line at a Polish supermarket as the transition to a free market economy got under way. This market was still a state-owned and -operated enterprise, but was surrounded by a free marketplace. Out in the marketplace, just about everything from Levis to home-cured pickles was available. The independent peddlers made their offerings from fancy stalls, from open tables, from the backs of cars and trucks. The realities of supply and demand controlled the prices, and they were high.

But inside the state-subsidized store, there were still bargains. The prices were controlled. The selection was pitiful, the quality marginal, but the prices were low. It was at that store that I came face-to-face with the shopping basket rule. Stacks of hand-carried wire baskets greet shoppers at all East bloc state-run stores. Enforced custom forbids coming into the store without one of these baskets. This means that when the store gets crowded and the basket supply is exhausted, no one can come into the store until someone leaves and frees up a shopping basket.

If you arrive at such a store unfamiliar with the rule and just walk in, you are attacked by at least one clerk and harangued as if you surely must be a thief. The disjointed logic seems to be that carrying the basket precludes shoplifting.

The Polish transition from a centrally planned economy to one controlled by supply and demand was called shock therapy because of the almost overnight elimination of subsidies and price controls. Unemployment hit hard, as unprofitable businesses went under and featherbedding employees lost their jobs. When Poles gritted their teeth and accepted the suddenly increasing hardships in their lives, it wasn't just a testimonial to how much support the Solidarity-controlled government enjoyed, it was also an indication of just how motivated they were to free themselves of domination by the Communist government and its policies and philosophies.

The editor of the English-language Warsaw newspaper *The Warsaw Voice* tried to clarify the optimistic mood in a March 1990 editorial, three months into the "shock therapy."

"For many years in Poland," wrote Andrzej Jonas, "when trips to the West were still a great rarity and a negative opinion about the West obligatory, the following joke was being told: after returning from England, a certain gentleman was pestered by his friends. They wanted to know what it was like there and if it was true that capitalism was dying. 'Yes,' he said, 'it's true, but what a beautiful death.' A similar thing is happening in Poland today," explained Jonas. "The whole country is in crisis, difficulties are mounting, and there's still no sign of improvement. But people say: what marvelous prospects we've got, despite the crisis."

★   ★   ★

Poland's relationship to West Germany is like Nevada's to California. Nevada is a playground for Californians; Nevadans dip into California to scoop out some of the excess wealth.

Since travel restrictions were dropped for Poles, a common sight on West German highways is cars with Polish plates towing a junk car with West German plates back toward Poland. An old, funky Mercedes pulls a newer, crashed Mercedes. These throwaways from the rich West German culture are on their way to Poland to be cannibalized for parts or rebuilt as cruisers. The West Germans might have all the money, but the Poles make good use of their leftovers.

★   ★   ★

Balding middle-aged Stefan Borowiak runs a private store selling household goods and furniture. He stops by Grzegoz and Lucynna's apartment for morning coffee. Since the change in government, customers cannot afford to buy from him. He says he will stay open until the end of the month and then close. What's next for him? A regular job if he's lucky, at a tiny wage, or unemployment. Would he trade his previous successful business for a return to the old oppressive system? An adamant "No!" The same answer I heard over and over again to that question, just as I heard over and over again a continuing sense of hope and expectation that the future will be brighter and that the Polish people can make it through this period of transition.

Then he and Lucynna talked for a couple of minutes in rapid Polish.

She smiled at me and translated:

"We have this proposition, we three. We want to have a war with the United States. And from—one day is the war—and from tomorrow [she looks up the word in the dictionary] we surrender!"

Stefan chimes in, in Polish, "It's the only way."

"And from tomorrow," smiles Lucynna, "everything in Poland will be better."

In the background, Tina Turner screams on Radio Three.

Chapter Five

CULTURED CZECHS AND
DIRTY SLOVAKS

"If not now, when? If not us, who?"

—Banner in Wenceslas Square, November 1989

IN THE COLD, damp November of 1989, hundreds of thousands of Czechs and Slovaks were gathering after work every night in Wenceslas Square to hear speakers insist on the need to overthrow the government. The second day after I arrived in Prague the Communist regime was still threatening to resort to force to stay in power. All through that day we watched bus loads of Communist militia troops being transported from the provinces to the capital. They sped through the streets under police escort. These special soldiers looked tough and grim, filling the buses, staring like strangers out through the windows at the rebellious city. And they *were* strangers, brought in from the provinces precisely because they were loyal to the Party and without allegiance to the intellectuals in the capital city. It was clear that the buses were crisscrossing the city not just to deploy the troops but also to parade them in public, making a clear show of force as a scare tactic.

But that evening the crowd in Wenceslas Square was even bigger than the night before. And as the night's speeches ended, hundreds of thousands of Czechs and Slovaks held their house and car keys high in the air and shook them. The message was a symbolic locking out of the old rulers. The clinking of the keys reverberated across the square. For a few minutes there was no other sound. This subtle power was a strong match psychologically for the bus loads of soldiers. Finally, the haunting national anthem was sung in perfect unison by the huge crowd.

Through moments like that rally, Markos and I were escorted by a Czech biochemist and revolutionary who decided to take us on as his personal responsibility. It was an incredibly lucky encounter for us. We had just arrived in Prague as one of the first rallies was coming to an end earlier in the week. We joined the crowd as it adjourned, moving down the square. Markos glanced at the baseball cap on a fellow walking next to us. The slogan San Francisco Drinking Club stitched into the cap looked out of place there in Prague, but it was English in a foreign port. We didn't know where we were going to spend that night, or much about what was happening. We didn't know anyone in the whole city.

"You must speak English!" Markos announced to the baseball cap guy.

The blank look he received back was that all-too-familiar one that let us know immediately we were not communicating.

But a fellow walking right next to him sang out, "I do!"

That's how we ended up with our biochemist guide, Jan Konvalinka, for the next three days. Jan led us everywhere, translating everything.

★   ★   ★

That first evening in Prague Jan took us to the Prague Academy of Fine Arts, where his wife was a student now on strike. The entrance was locked and guarded as we arrived. We were scrutinized by the student sentry, as our new friend explained who we were.

Banners and Czech flags covered the facade of the Academy, just one of the university buildings that had been occupied by striking students since riot police attacked a student march the week before. The brutality of the unprovoked police assault became the catalyst for the movement that eventually forced the Communist dictators from power in Czechoslovakia. Students initially obtained permission for a march to commemorate a student demonstration against fascism that was held in 1939. But then without official authorization, thousands of the marchers headed toward the center of Prague and Wenceslas Square. On Národní Street a wall of police stopped the parade. The demonstrators offered flowers and candles; the police attacked with their batons.

A reporter for the official Czechoslovak News Agency was on the scene the night of the police attack to observe for himself what was going on, not to write a report. "I was not allowed to. In such cases we waited for the Interior Ministry and an official version approved at the highest levels." But later, after the revolution, he told his story in a summary of the revolution published by the post-Communist official news agency:

> Most horrible was probably a moment of total silence with an echo of police orders coming from afar, and the stamping of hobnailed boots. Girls put flowers on the shields of the young men in helmets, and the front lines of the sitting demonstrators were protecting themselves with lighted candles. They were sure no attack would come; after all, the date was November 17.
>
> Then it happened. Suddenly we were being pressed together. Nobody knew what was happening; we only heard ironic orders to disperse. Somebody fell down, there were cries of fear and horror. I saw from the arcade men in uniform; their faces were purple and they were beating indiscriminately.[1]

Markos and I arrived less than a week after the police riot. The student strike had shut down schools across the country, and efforts were under way to convince factory workers to join the students on strike.

"We want freedom" and "Don't fight evil with violence," declared the signs strung over the front of the art academy.

Long-haired students in blue jeans and sweaters jam the lobby. A black-and-white portable television drones. Coffee, tea, and cigarettes keep the strikers going. Most have slept only a few hours since November 17.

---

[1]The review of the 1989 revolution from the perspective of the liberated government news agency can be found at the Czechoslovak News Agency foreign services desk, Opletalova 5, 111 44 Prague 1.

In a meeting room, the walls covered with modern art, a twenty-three-year-old sculpture student, Ludek Radl, gathered with the strike committee and acted as their spokesman.

"The main purpose," he tells us, explaining the strike, "is for the government to resign." Before answering each question, he consults with the rest of the committee. They discuss and debate and agree on a response.

"We are persuaded," he says, "that Friday's event was just the last drop in our lifelong living a lie."

Most of the art school strikers were on the streets when the police attacked. One of them, Martin Frind, pulls up his shirt to show his bruised back. He was kicked by police and says he wants the government to resign immediately. Like many of the revolutionary students, he is intent on change but isn't sure what will or should replace the system that's been in power since the Prague Spring, finessed by Alexander Dubcek, was crushed by Soviet troops in 1968.

Then he says with a laugh, "It doesn't matter; anything would be better than this one!"

Unlike the thousands of East Germans who simply fled to the West before the Berlin Wall opened, these Czech students are intent on taking their country back from the Communist elite. "We are tired of being scared," says Radl. It is a slow, measured, deliberate announcement.

The exhausted student leader is wearing a jacket over his shoulders for warmth. Two days' growth of beard add to his revolutionary demeanor.

"I'm not scared at all." His English is slow, but clear. "I am not scared at all, because yesterday I joined a demonstration and it made me feel much stronger. There's no doubt the whole nation will support us."

These are brave words and turn out to be prophetic. But in those early days of the Czechoslovakian revolution, there was no guarantee that the student movement would succeed. Certainly not all Czechs were actively supporting the resistance. One forty-year-old hotel cook, who said she was on the streets sup-

porting Dubcek's reforms in 1968, insisted she could not afford
to demonstrate this time.

Eating lunch in a café overlooking Wenceslas Square, she
asked, "Who will take care of my baby if I am killed?" She had
seen the bus loads of troops on the streets and feared that,
despite government promises not to use violence against the
mass demonstrations in the square, soldiers would be used to
break up demonstrations.

"You can't trust the Communists," she grunted in disgust.

* * *

The art students use the school's equipment to print posters
decorated with a flower, the national colors, and the legends
"Free Elections" and "Democracy to the Republic."

"We put them on walls around the city," says Anna Neborova,
her eyes fiery. "And immediately some people pulled them down
and were furious. Other people said, 'Put them back.' We said,
'Let them be and put up your own posters.' But they didn't want
to discuss anything."

Most of the posters, fliers, and newsletters stayed on the
walls. They are plastered on many Prague street corners, drawing, in the light falling snow, crowds of people long unac-
customed to reading dissident literature in public.

Through these early days of revolution, candles burn at
statues of national heroes. Except for striking students, actors,
and museum workers, regular work continues until the crowd
gathers in the square in the late afternoon to show support for
student demands.

"We're going to be here until the government resigns," insists
Radl. He is collecting videotapes delivered to the art school for
the students to watch to help divert them from their worry
about an attack by police late in the night.

All this revolutionary action makes Jan ecstatic. "The country
is going to hell finally!" he smiles, watching enthusiastically as
protesters chant, sing, cheer, honk car horns, light candles, and
wave the Czechoslovakian flag. "Everybody was waiting for a
signal, and the violence of the police was that signal."

Konvalinka was whipped on the back with a riot policeman's stick during that first demonstration. He is convinced that the government will fall in just a few days (rightly, as it turns out).

"Communism without violence cannot survive," he insists.

"Communism for the Communists!" is one of the demonstrators' chants out on the street. "Forty years is enough!" is another. Still another is a rhyme that bounces through the crowd. "Leaders must be retired!" starts the yell. "Leaders should become shovelers!" another group answers. "Leaders are not worthy of shovels!" is the next response. And then, "Leaders would steal the shovels!"—the final retort.

Over and over again demonstrators say they are no longer afraid of the government. Indeed, it appears that the government is beginning to fear the masses in the streets and so made its promise not to use troops against the demonstrators.

"We don't know what will happen next," acknowledges a demonstrator as the crowd around him chants.

But Konvalinka thinks he knows what will happen. "You know the old fairy tale about the king with no clothes?" he asks with a smile. "Now the people shout 'No clothes!'"

*   *   *

Jan Konvalinka turned out to be not just a thorough guide and translator but an accurate forecaster of the direction the revolution would take over the next few days. We walked through the dispersing crowd that first night we met him, and he talked about the changes he was seeing in his country.

"It is something very strange here. People are scared. But the police attack on the students was like a signal. It moved the people. The Communist system—nobody believes it. Where are the police? They are scared."

It was all happening so fast, without a blueprint. But Jan was satisfied. "Probably the government will go away. There will be new elections. Nobody knows how. Of course it is because of Gorbachev. And the DDR revolution was very important. When the people just go to the streets and protest for several days, the system is not strong enough to survive it. Our leaders are extremely stupid."

By this time we had walked across the magical town center, virtually undamaged during World War II. A trip through Staromestske namesti, the old town square, with its perfectly preserved baroque palaces, is an overwhelming experience the first few times. The ornate decorations glimmer on the buildings; there's no motorized traffic on the cobblestone streets. Hushed voices echo between walls that were standing when only Indians lived in America. Even without a revolution going on, Staromestske namesti is thrilling.

But that night, added to the glistening gilt of the Old Town Hall, the Saint Nicholas Church, and the Tyn Church, was the excited murmur of the revolutionary crowd breaking up. People made their way home or to bars and cafés as they contemplated the overthrow of their oppressors and discussed tactics for the coming days.

The Czechoslovakian revolution is called the velvet revolution because it was so smooth and without violence. But the softness was also in the physical atmosphere. It was not just that the people rid themselves of the dictators without the street fighting that came a month later in Romania. There was a sensual quality to the Czechoslovakian revolution that made the term *velvet revolution* particularly appropriate. That sensuality came in part from the storybook streets of Prague where the revolution took place. It came, too, from the demeanor of the revolutionaries.

On a side street I found a wild-looking man with a can of red spray paint. He was wearing a long overcoat with the collar turned up and had a messy beard. He was scrawling support for Civic Forum on a wall. Such political graffiti was then a serious crime. But he was taking his time, being careful. He was writing his message on a piece of plywood that covered a broken window, making sure that he did not deface the historic building.

* * *

My pen was running out of ink and all the stores were closed. Jan insisted that Markos and I go with him to his brother's apartment, where there would be a pen to use and we could watch how the government-controlled television was dealing with events.

That night, the TV showed pictures of the demonstration. A student was interviewed saying, "We are not satisfied." Such acknowledgment of dissent on the official TV news was unprecedented. The newscasters tried to compensate for the pictures of hundreds of thousands of demonstrators by airing an interview with the prime minister.

"We need political reforms; we will speak to the people," the Communist prime minister told the audience. "But," and it was clear the Communists were completely out of touch with what was happening on the streets, "we will protect socialism. Students will not be attacked. Go back to schools. Go back to theaters."

It was too little, too late.

* * *

After three days, events died down long enough for us to consider a quiet dinner, and we invited Jan along as our guest. As we had for the last three days, we pumped him for answers to our questions.

"Our leaders are so stupid," he kept repeating.

He ate a hearty portion of ham, then ate mine, too (meat that the waiter had mistakenly brought me). On his biochemist's salary he could afford meat only every two weeks.

* * *

But finally, we realized we had a responsibility to do more than ask questions and fill our Czech friend full of ham.

"We've been asking you questions for three days," we said; "now it's your turn. What do you want to know about us? What do you want to know about America and Americans?"

The response came without malice, and it was not without precedent. We heard similar complaints and queries throughout our European travels.

"Why are Americans so undereducated?" asked Jan. "Why are Americans so uncultured, so superficial?"

Despite their fascination with American popular culture, with the grandeur of the North American continent, with the American version of the English language, Jan and many European intellectuals I've met over the years remain convinced that Americans are not their equals. It is always irritating to be on the receiving end of such an arrogant assessment of American intellectual prowess.

I tried hard with Jan—as I usually do when this charge arises—to defend Americans as intellectually on a par with the rest of the world. "Look," I said, "there can be different, yet just as valuable, types of culture and education. Who is to say that an American automobile mechanic, who can tear an engine apart and rebuild it and knows all about rock and roll, is any less sophisticated than his Czech counterpart just because his grasp of European history might be weak?"

Mine is a thin argument, especially when Jan points out correctly that the Czech mechanic probably knows just as much about Elvis Presley and cowboys and Indians as the American, and speaks at least three languages, plays Beethoven, and holds at least one advanced degree. I now tend to limit my response to this intellectual form of anti-Americanism by citing a survey that showed most British schoolchildren identified Salman Rushdie as a fish.

*   *   *

"I'd rather be a bag lady!"

That was my wife Sheila's response when I suggested that life would be difficult if we decided to move to my great-grand-father's roadhouse in the village of Nizna Orava. We had just traveled across Czechoslovakia, making our way into the Tatra Mountains. We had finally located the old Slovakian family homestead.

We were a few miles away, in the closest city with available lodgings, staying in the best hotel in Dolby Kubin. The Hotel Severin sign on the roof of the hotel was plastic. Each letter was a plastic bubble attached to the building, and most were cracked or completely shattered. It was clear that the plastic had broken a long time ago and no one had any intention of fixing the letters.

From the street the hotel looked closed, maybe deserted. The broken letters on the sign only added to the desolation. But experience in the Eastern bloc taught us to expect business as usual behind dark, abandoned-looking doors and windows. The parking lot was almost empty, too—just a couple of Russian Moskas, and a Czech Škoda or two.

We walked up the concrete steps, opened the metal-frame doors. The concrete was maybe ten, at the most twenty, years old, but it was already crumbling because of lack of maintenance and the poor quality of the materials used. The same was true for the metal-frame doors; they were rusting, dirty, ill fitting.

Inside was a darkened reception lounge, with a pudgy woman behind the counter. This lobby was lit by one stark fluorescent tube. On a desk the TV was blaring in Slovakian. It was the weather forecast in black and white with a few shadows and some snow. The TV itself was bright red; that was the only color in the room.

"Do you speak English?" The answer was no, but German worked, as it does with the older generation throughout Eastern Europe. We convinced her to give up the key so we could take a look at the room. Three beds, a bathroom, a balcony with a view of the Orava River: one hundred ninety-five crowns. At the official exchange rate, that comes to about twelve dollars. That's at the official exchange rate. For each day in the country at that time, each adult had to exchange about fifteen dollars at the primary artificial exchange rate of about sixteen crowns to the dollar. Further exchanges could be made if you wanted to spend more money, at the noncompulsory official rate of about twenty-four crowns to the dollar. On the street, the black market brought much more. The people have plenty of crowns. What they need is hard currency so they can travel and buy things not available in Czechoslovakia.

Certainly twelve bucks for three to stay in the best hotel in town is a bargain. But the room was just on the bearable side of filthy.

Gray, depressing Slovakia is the epitome of the post-Communist nightmare, especially compared with Vienna, whose opulence is an alarming contrast. Strategically placed just a hop from Eastern European capitals, Vienna is a useful place for travelers working behind the remnants of the Iron Curtain to dip into the West to take care of business. It almost hurts the eyes to see all the wealth that's displayed in Vienna's shop windows. The subway stations are more luxurious than most homes in the East. The stores drip with merchandise unavailable in the East, from electronics to fruits and vegetables.

In Vienna we used the Visa machine to get more cash in hard Austrian shillings. We bought the *International Herald Tribune* to find out what had been going on in the rest of the world and sent mail off to America. What takes weeks from Eastern Europe gets home in just a few days from Vienna.

Then we made our way down the Danube toward Bratislava and into Czechoslovakia. The old Communist government had been out of office through the winter. Václav Havel was interim president. The outlook was hopeful, but many of the old rules remained in effect.

The shock was severe leaving Austria and heading into Czechoslovakia. The border was no longer much of a problem, though the irritating rules remained. You couldn't simply pick up the needed visa at the border but were forced to get it at an embassy or a mission in some other country. It was expensive, and Czechoslovakia still mandated that you change money at the official rate for every day that you spent in the country. The rules were complex and involved plenty of paperwork. But even at the official exchange rate, Czechoslovakia was an incredible bargain. It was hard to spend more than a few dollars at any restaurant. Despite the low prices, the black market was active.

As in East Germany, Poland, and Hungary by 1990, people enjoyed the political freedom to travel. Many of them were equipped with more than enough crowns to pay their bills with piles left over, but they could not exchange their money for hard Western currency. So they still were unable to travel. They still could not buy the Western goods that were previously denied to them for political reasons. Consequently, they looked for opportunities to gather hard currency. One easy method was to exchange money on the black market. Another was to offer goods and services for Western currency. Renting rooms to tourists for hard currency became a convenient avenue to earn valuable foreign money.

With just a cursory check this time by the customs police, we went on into the sprawl of Bratislava. After the bucolic scenery of Austria, the change is hard to deal with. The dominant color is suddenly brown. There is grit, garbage and all sorts of debris in the streets. Blocks of apartments that look like the South Bronx cover the Danube hillsides. Smokestacks fill the skyline.

Except for a theater here and a palace there — lucky remnants of a richer past — Bratislava is one more crumbling, depressing, Communist-ruined city to get out of quickly. There was a freeway — hated by the locals for bisecting the old downtown with cars and concrete — to get out of town quickly, and we headed north on it toward the Tatra Mountains and my great-grandfather's farmhouse.

The farmhouse is a family memory. I remember stories from my father about the good times he had playing there as a child. There's one crackly old black-and-white photograph that circulates through the family of my father and his grandfather and some other members of the family gathered around in front of the house. An image of the facade of the place is ingrained in my mind, combined with my fantasies conjured up from those stories.

We're not alone in holding some faraway property. One of the results of the fall of Communism in the East is a reawakening of interest in the private property confiscated from or left behind by the millions who escaped when the Communists took over. Now, many of those property owners who left their homes and farms behind as they rushed West, and many others who did not leave but still lost their property to state confiscation, want the land and buildings returned. All through the Eastern bloc title searches are under way. One of the messier negotiating difficulties facing the emerging governments in the East is figuring out how to deal with the overlapping interests of those who lost their land, buildings, and businesses and those who took over and developed the land seized by the Communists. One West German lawyer handling these types of cases suggests that in Germany alone as many as a million people could legitimately make property claims.

Title was pretty straightforward for our family. I sat down with a cousin in Budapest and went through the thick file he kept on the property. Paperwork from the last century clearly established that the farmhouse was still in our family. There were some complications: My Hungarian cousin had signed over his part to a relative in America for safekeeping during the forties, when the new Communist government in Czechoslovakia passed a law making it illegal for Hungarians to own property in Czechoslovakia.

But the problems were within the family, not with the government. There was a state-owned grocery store renting the old place from us. Every month they paid the family some rent into a Czechoslovakian crown account. After about twenty years, my cousin had figured the total was around a thousand American dollars.

So we were on the freeway heading north, hungry, on the way to check out this farm. About twenty-five miles outside Bratislava, the freeway ends. There's a crossroads town a few more miles along and a sign for a restaurant. There's a parking lot. There's a motel. It looks like a crossroads in Kansas or Nebraska at first glance.

But nothing can really prepare the traveling Californian for the accommodations. It's certainly not that I'm particularly squeamish. I've seen filth all over India, eaten at a Pakistani restaurant where the floor was dirt and the chicken too scrawny to bother with, shared yucca root and eggs with Bolivian farmers in tin shacks filled with flies. But in those situations, I felt less shocked than I did encountering the miserable eateries in Eastern Europe—like the place where we ate lunch that day. I expected difficulty in places like Bolivia and Pakistan. I expected strange conditions. I was prepared for culture shock because those cultures are so different from my own, from top to bottom.

The degradation of Eastern Europe is so depressing because the culture is essentially the same as our own. It was thriving and sophisticated when America was still engaged in Indian wars and the West was wild. But the one-two punch of the Nazis and the Communists set these countries into a tailspin that will take years to overcome.

Where to start with this poor restaurant? The physical building itself, perhaps: dirty, caked with layers of dust and grime on the floors, window sills, and curtains. The curtains were lace and white when they were first hung. That was probably more than twenty years before, and it looked as if they had not been washed since; the yellow-brown dirt was now simply part of the curtains. The tablecloth, too, was stained and dirty, with no attempt made to clean it. Not just our table, but all the tables were covered with dirty cloths. The wallpaper was fading and peeling, a nondescript pattern and dirty. The colors throughout were institutional grays, browns, oranges — depressing colors.

The decor was Spartan, just tables and chairs and an old fifties jukebox against one wall. Nothing matched; nothing looked inviting; nothing looked appetizing. On the contrary, everything looked about as unappetizing as imaginable. The windows were dirty; the bathroom was filthy.

The waiter came to the table, and though it probably wasn't his fault that he had fallen off his motorcycle (or something) he added to the bleak picture. His face was scratched up and scabby; his eyes were hollow and uninterested.

If you have no experience with Slavic languages — and we had none — then a menu in Slovakian is pretty useless. But the waiter tried to help us through it, and then brought a stained, ragged copy in German.

The alternative to eating meat was scrambled eggs — the second of three meals of scrambled eggs I'd eat that day.

Back on the road, we moved up into the foothills on a two-lane road. The weather soured, turning gray. It drizzled. But the countryside looked promising.

★   ★   ★

Ahead were the Tatra Mountains. The guidebooks list them as some of the prettiest mountains in Eastern Europe. I'd spent time studying the maps of the region, checking out the topography. It looked as though it could be spectacular, nestled up against the Polish border, in the Orava River valley. I saw an old black-and-white photograph in a Hungarian picture book about the Tatras. The village of Nizna Orava looked quaint and appealing.

There was one ominous warning that the little village might be in the midst of the environmental disaster created by Communist developers in parts of the Tatras. My cousin had drawn a map of the village, pinpointing just where the old house was located. One of his landmarks was the Tesla television factory.

We climbed north, past names that were so foreign it was hard to look at the road signs and remember the spelling long enough to find them on the map: Zilina, Karl'ovany, Dolby Kubin. With practically each bend of the river, the view of pine forests on the mountainsides was interrupted by blocks of apartment buildings—ugly, enormous blocks of apartments, built maybe twenty years ago and aging poorly. Once white or whitish, they were dirty, pieces of the concrete facades missing—scars on the landscape.

The apartment blocks were built on such an unwieldy scale that there was no getting away from looking at them as huge ruins, ruins that covered the landscape but were still in use. It was as if we were looking at the evidence of a culture gone wrong that was still in existence: current archaeology.

Next to these oversized masses of accommodation, each bunch of blocks holding thousands of people, were the factories where the workers—it was hard to think of them as anything other than prisoned inmates—worked. The poisoned smoke belched from the factories, drifting lazily over the living quarters and what was left of the landscape.

The gray drizzle didn't help our response and mood, but even on a sunny day the rape of the Orava Valley would have dominated our impressions.

Finally we approached my great-grandfather's village. It was like all the rest we had seen along the way: dirty, the few old picturesque houses left dominated by the crud all around, by the faded sixties architecture of the sprawling TV factory. It was not picturesque, not appealing, not a place to even consider spending the night, let alone a vacation, or a life.

The sickening sweet stench of brown coal filled the valley. Fat peasant women, babushkas on their heads, were out in the fields with the gnarled old men, plows pulled by horses, doing the spring planting.

On the main drag we found the house. It was impossible to mistake for any other. We had the old photo for reference, and the facade was the same. We could tell by the placement of the windows and doors, the proportions of the building. There was no other quite like it of that vintage in the village. The front was the common dirty mustard color.

The Potriviny was closed, but we looked in the window of the state-run market. It was like all the other state groceries, the fading labels of the same old stuff on the shelves. This week it was pineapple juice from Vietnam (the brand that won at the 1975 Leipzig trade fair), jugs of apricot preserves, plastic bags of milk, powdered soups.

The old building is still divided in half. My great-grandfather had lived in one half and used the other side as a pub. The part that's not a grocery store was now being renovated, new tile being installed. It was impossible to tell what was being put into the place — maybe another pub. I tried to work up some enthusiasm for the house. Trucks barreled by just inches from the front door on the main road. In the old family photo, the main road was a dirt track; the romance of the old stories was just not there.

Out in back, the old barn was a ruin, empty and barely standing. We took some pictures and waved a sad good-bye. Our dreams of resurrecting the ancestral farm and turning it into a European hideaway were wrecked by the reality of the post-Communist rural devastation.

Next stop was for *pivo* — hearty, strong Czechoslovakian beer.

★   ★   ★

The *pivo* stop was two villages back down the river. It was a carbon copy of the grimy place we had stopped at for lunch. The metal frame on the door was corroding. The government-issue curtains, which the central office in Prague in charge of curtains must have ordered for all the bars and restaurants in Czechoslovakia, were stained and dirty. The stark wooden tables were littered with tired old men drinking *pivo*. The bartender stood behind his tapper pulling the beers. Next to the tap was a sink full of stagnant water; washing glasses meant slopping them through the still water. The glasses were cracked and chipped, the windows cracked, the paint peeling.

It is impossible to overemphasize the miserable grimness of the place, the depressing grayness, the lack of spirit. There was no human concern evident to keep the place from being a pigsty. It wasn't that it was just messy, or even just messy and dirty. What was sobering and saddening was to realize that no one seemed to mind anymore how messy and dirty the place was, and no one cared about the lack of concern.

★   ★   ★

The barkeep came over to the table next to ours with a rag. He swiped at the sticky tablecloth with the filthy rag and smeared the crud around.

One *pivo* was enough. We made our way out in search of lodging for the night.

That's when we found Dolby Kubin, one of the monstrosities built by the Communists. The town has been there forever. But it's only in the last twenty years or so that the blocks of crumbling apartment houses were thrown up on the hillsides. That's when the Severin Hotel went up, too, the one with the fluorescent tube flickering in the lobby, where we rented the twelve-dollar room. The hotel where the toilet moved sideways when you sat on it — not the toilet seat, the whole toilet. The place with the cigarette burns covering the carpet, with the broken glass panel separating the balcony from the next room's balcony. The corridors were empty and dark, the only sign of life some giggling from women in the room right next door.

The desk clerk sent us to a restaurant up the street.

"Go upstairs, the food is better. Don't go to the Hotel Orava; the food isn't too good."

But that's where we ended up, because the other restaurant was closed. Like all the bars, hotels, and restaurants, the Orava was dirty. The lamps hanging from the ceiling were skewed at odd angles, chipped, and cracked. The glasses were chipped, too. Windows were broken, paint peeling. This time there was no German-language menu. Nothing on the Slovakian one suggested to us what was available, so we drew pictures on napkins of fish and salad. But the waitress shook her head. Then she came back with a slightly pickled fellow carrying a binder full of papers.

"What do you want?" The English was heavily accented — and quite a relief.

"Anything without meat." It's tough to be a vegetarian traveling through Eastern Europe.

"Eggs?" That sounded fine to us. We had already made it that far with the waitress by drawing ovals, flapping our arms, and squawking.

Shortly the plates arrived with some sort of omelet filled with potatoes and the usual pickled cucumbers and cabbage that's called salad.

As we ate, we bought our translator wine. He drank, smoked Sheila's cigarettes, got drunker, and told us he was "dissident!"

He crossed his hands and said he was "three years in prison, politics school."

We asked him what he did for a living?

"Politics," he waved his binder. "Petitions."

This land is so sad, he said. "Ruined by the Communists. The air, the water."

He shook his head, sank into his seat.

After the third or fourth time around, I tried to change the subject. It wasn't that I didn't want to talk politics with the fellow, but the limited common language between us, combined with his drunkenness, was getting him more and more morose and frustrated, and I was looking for a way to bring him back out of his depression.

I wrote some basic words on a piece of napkin and asked him for the Slovakian translations. Eat. No meat. Please. Thank you. Hello.

When I got to "How much does it cost?" he shook his drunken head and scowled. "No," he just kept saying. Finally he just wrote in English next to my words, "Nothing," and made it clear that what he meant was that we didn't need to learn how to ask the price of anything, because we would not find anything in Slovakia that we would want to buy.

As ten o'clock approached, the restaurant was closing. We got up to go, and our political activist made his move. He thrust his petition at me and told me to sign it "for Slovakia."

I explained to him that I could not sign his petition without knowing what was written on it. Sheila just wanted to make the poor fellow happy, pointing out quite correctly to me that it really made no difference what I was signing up there in the middle of nowhere.

But I decided to make the guy translate. And word for word he went through the petition's demands for high schools to stop teaching ethnic Hungarians in the Hungarian language.

Here it was just a few months after the dictatorship had been overthrown. He was free to get drunk, not work, circulate a petition. The countryside was devastated from pollution, the economy barely functioning. And this guy was busying himself trying to keep the local Hungarians from studying in Hungarian.

I made him retranslate a couple of times to make sure I had it right. I asked him what he wanted the name of his country to become, and he wrote out on the napkin not just the hyphenated Czecho-Slovakia with the capitalized S that the Slovakian nationals were pushing for, but Czecho&Slovakia.

After seeing the mess made of my great-grandfather's village, I wasn't in the mood to sign any petitions against my Hungarian ancestry. I wrote out at the bottom of his petition, "I oppose any suppression of the Slovakian language," and signed my name.

The problem with this dissident was not just that he wanted to keep the Hungarians from studying in Hungarian. Sheila was anxious to sign his petition because she felt sorry for him. She wanted to make him happy. But he didn't ask her for her signature, only for her cigarettes. Even after I signed my name on his paper, all he did was thank me over and over again, and we walked out of the hotel. Especially up in the Slovakian hills, postrevolutionary Czechoslovakia is still a sexist society. He wasn't interested in a woman's signature on his petition.

★   ★   ★

It's all changing so fast. This interim period keeps people worrying. They want to expect that everything will improve, but they've seen such hard times that they're nervous. Many of the old laws are still on the books. These repressive laws are not being enforced, but there is still fear that they could be enforced again. About six months after the velvet revolution, Sheila and I made our way to Prague to witness the social evolution that followed. We rented a flat in a working-class district. From the kitchen window, I look out at the first private grocery store to open in the city since the Communist government fell. It is Sunday. Everything else in town is shut up tight, but the market is doing a booming business, with a crowd lined up out front. A van pulls up to sell bread, and another line forms.

On the streets and highways, cars scream along at breakneck speed, grabbing at the chance to worry less about the police. There's a new striptease show downtown. The radio is blaring with a French station beaming in from Paris on satellite. Like Radio Bridge in Budapest, the new station that airs Voice of America newscasts, this Prague broadcast is a brand-new service. So much is changing so fast it's just about impossible to keep up with what's new.

We went back to the Albatross Hotel to visit the woman who had risked her bartending job to march and attend the November revolutionary rallies. "I had to," she had said at the time, "I have a six-year-old daughter."

She had looked so hurt when she told us about the police riot that provoked the revolution. "I saw a girl give flowers to a policeman and he hit her . . ."

But now, months later, her sad eyes brightened when we showed up at the bar; her life was improving. She was considering a hotel job in England, now that she could travel. Her daughter was studying English.

The changes were occurring so rapidly in Czechoslovakia it became a game trying to keep track of them. The radical Westernization and modernization was pretty much limited to Prague. But the pace was dizzying.

★ ★ ★

I returned again six months later in November 1990 for still another look around just in time for the celebration of the first anniversary of the revolution. This time I stayed at Petr's apartment, the same apartment that Markos and I had used as a base when the streets were jammed with hundreds of thousands of Czechoslovakians overthrowing the dictators. Back then, we came off the streets after the nightly demonstrations, and Petr would study the evening news reports offered by the government monopoly television station. Then he would wait on the telephone for the opportunity to get hold of a programmer at the TV operation to harangue him or her about their lopsided reporting of the evening's events. Calls like Petr's eventually encouraged the TV reporters and producers to show the rest of Czechoslovakia what was really happening in Wenceslas Square by reporting the nightly demonstrations live.

Now we were sitting in his kitchen watching the news again. This time it's CNN broadcasting into his apartment live from Atlanta. "What can I get you?" I ask him the question automatically, as I'm about to leave Prague for a week. A year before such a question would elicit a list of important goods unavailable in Prague, from chocolate to soft toilet paper. "Nothing," Petr smiles, "we have everything."

And, indeed, that's how it feels in Prague.

Just getting into the country is entirely different. Instead of a long, harassing border check after an expensive and laborious pre-trip visa expedition, a fat and smiling Czech border guard just stamps my passport (free) and a customs guy just waves me in without even glancing into my car.

The loudspeakers are mostly gone from the light poles in the villages between the German border and Prague; sometimes just bare wires remain from where people ripped them out. The loudspeakers had been used to force patriotic music and government directives into people's lives.

Individual private enterprise is at work. An old Trabbie is parked conspicuously on the edge of the city with a bright light shining on the home-made sign filling a side window: *Privat Zimmer Frei*, Private Room Available. It's late at night. Prague is getting famous for its shortage of hotel rooms. The Trabbie driver is waiting for a late, rich German without reservations. Overnight accommodations are going for two hundred dollars.

The dilapidated streetcars rattle along, rusted, badly in need of paint and extensive bodywork. Then one shows up, speeding toward Wenceslas Square, that actually seems to be riding higher on the tracks, presenting itself proudly. The paint is brand-new, and the tram looks good, even with the huge British Airways ad that's boldly part of the new look.

It's not all good news. There's a new lock on the lobby door leading up to Petr's apartment. Crime in Prague is increasing, officially up by 40 percent since the revolution. Petty criminals enjoyed an amnesty, others received sentence reductions, and there was no wholesale purge of the standing police forces. The new government needed police, but the cops are slacker in discharging their duties, taking a wait-and-see attitude. It's a combination of the change in mentality — police harassment is not being tolerated — and the fact that the police themselves are trying to figure out their role in the new society. They do not yet feel allegiance to the new regime.

The conflict between the Slovaks and the Czechs continues. Finally, after hunger strikes and threats of secession, a language law is passed that pacifies the Slovaks. It makes Slovakian the only official language in Slovakia but allows minorities who live there to use their own languages. Some of the extreme Slovakian nationalists continue to want Hungarians and other minorities living in Slovakia prevented from conducting official business in any other language.

The name of the country is finally determined. The Slovaks, feeling deprived of worldwide recognition with the name Czechoslovakia, resist even the compromise Czecho-Slovakia. The Slovaks remain convinced that foreigners usually do not realize that the Slovaks are a separate nationality with a separate republic within the federation. Such a worry is fueled by the cultural differences between Czechs and Slovaks.

"I don't like Slovaks; they're so dirty," the barmaid at the Albatross had admitted. When I told Jan about the barmaid's comment, he put his arm around his Slovakian wife, gave her a squeeze, and smiled, "Dasha is not dirty." But then he was serious for a minute, saying the prejudice between the two nationalities is so severe that sometimes the two of them feel like an interracial couple.

The conflicts threaten to split the country, and Havel asks for and gets increased presidential powers to establish clearly the different roles of the federal government and the Czech and Slovak separate republics. "The state is not endangered from the outside, as has happened many times in the past," says Havel as he requests the new powers, "but from within. We are putting it at risk by our own lack of political culture, lack of democratic awareness and mutual understanding and . . . lack of experience."

Finally, at least the name change is resolved, and the country becomes the Czech and Slovak Federated Republic, still referred to around the world, of course, as Czechoslovakia.

All the petty bickering promotes jokes. Question: What will the new Europe be called once the East is part of it? Answer: The European Community and Slovakia.

Petr and Hanna live in a classic apartment building in the old section of Prague. Unlike the blocks of apartments built by the Communist government (government-owned or cooperatives) their building was in private hands when the Communists took power. The building was confiscated by the state, but soon, the surviving daughter of the owner who lost it to the government after the war, now in her seventies, will get the building back as personal property.

Civic Forum is orchestrating such returns of nationalized private property. It's good news for the heirs and the surviving property owners, but it means families like Petr, Hanna, and their little boy may well be forced to find a new place to live. Once their apartment—located in the heart of old Prague in a beautiful building—goes on the open market, the rent will skyrocket.

It's a tough job, trying to figure out how to right the overwhelming wrongs of recent history. In a statement of policy, the state-owned Czechoslovak News Agency explained simply, "Property will be returned to original owners or their heirs." But such a blanket pronouncement panicked Czechs living along the German border who had taken over land belonging to Sudeten Germans, Germans who moved across into West Germany after the Nazis were defeated. The Czechs feared a new invasion of Germans who would cross and take back the lands they abandoned after the war.

So, late in 1990 Civic Forum started explaining the rules, "We are not and will not be able to redress all the wrongs in our history. Easing the effects of wrongs or compensation cannot go beyond the date of the Communist coup on February 25, 1948." The cutoff date was designed to put an end to the demands of German nationalist organizations like Sudeten Landsmannschaft. After the revolution, the Sudeten Landsmannschaft demanded lands be returned to the Germans who moved after the war to "ensure the right of the individual to return on the basis of right to a homeland." Civic Forum dismissed such claims and rationalized the 1948 cutoff date on the basis that the West German government had already paid compensation to those Germans who moved into West Germany from the Sudetenland.

Everyone is feeling the way through this postrevolutionary period. But it clearly is a period of opportunity for those with the means and initiative to take a chance. Just a few months earlier, it was impossible to get an instant passport picture anywhere in

Prague. There was one store with a Polaroid passport picture machine, but it was broken. No one knew for sure when the repair would be completed; it just sat gathering dust while the clerk shrugged. Now the photo studio in the Museum subway station is just one of many spotted around town offering immediate service.

"To start a business is hard," explains one of the owners, Ladislau Krulich. He's young and hopeful, wearing a smile and a leather jacket as he waits for customers. There's paperwork to figure out, he says, paperwork that is made more difficult by the fact that nobody in the government knows exactly what new small businessmen should be doing as private enterprises start up.

But he and his partner harbor no doubts about their decision to go into business for themselves. "It is more interesting than working for the government. You can do more money than for the government." Krulich figures he's already making about four times what he'd pull in at a government job. But it's not just the money that lures them. "When it is yours, your business, you have a good feeling. When you work for the government, you could not see your results." It's a statement that pretty well sums up the draw of small private enterprise and the failings of centrally planned, state-owned economies. And Krulich is convinced he and his partner are not alone, "I think in Czechoslovakia when someone starts a business it will be good for him for money and feeling, and people will work hard."

Kotva, the department store, is jammed. It's not just Christmas shoppers. In January 1991, the prices will skyrocket, as subsidies disappear. But now, competing for the attention of bargain hunters accustomed to finding nothing more than poorly made Czechoslovakian toys are Legos and Barbie dolls. Kotva scurried to keep up with the demand. Czechoslovakians bought a thousand Barbies a day, once the doll became available.

Multinational companies deal with the confused and unpredictable situation by simply bypassing the Czechoslovakian economy. A brand-new car rental company opens in Prague, for example. The slick brochure features the glistening Mercedes

ALL PHOTOS BY PETER LAUFER

*In the shadow of the Reichstag, Turkish venders hawking Soviet and
East German military paraphernalia join entrepreneurial Germans
selling colored chips of the Berlin Wall encased in Plexiglas.*

One of the next generation of East Germans at a preunification
Leipzig election rally.

Just after the Wall fell, these East German boys found the no-man's-land between East and West a perfect backdrop for their gun play.

Personal property hidden away in East Germany, like this pristine antique car, appeared on the streets of West Berlin once the Wall fell. West Germans obtained treasures from the East German time capsule at bargain prices with hard currency.

Before it was torn down, the Checkpoint Charlie border crossing between East and West Berlin was left in ruins. A portion was salvaged and is on public display.

Advertising agencies were quick to take advantage of the liberated border between the two Germanys.

Grzegorz and Lucynna in front of their home in Poznan, Poland.

Arab money changers wait for their prey in the streets of Prague.

Memorial candles burn at a makeshift shrine in Wenceslas Square.

The line in front of the first post-Communist private grocery store to open in Prague. Within a year the private stores filled up with provisions long missing from Czechoslovakian dinner tables.

Hard currency only.

Immediately after the revolution, cultural opportunities in Czechoslovakia were virtually unlimited.

Old fears die hard in a rural Hungarian flea market.

Romanian cargo wagon.

Romanian sheepherder.

*Under Ceaușescu, Romanian traffic was restricted by police
stations on city borders. After the revolution, these symbols of
persecution became immediate targets and were destroyed.*

Farmers in Serbia.

*A year after the fall of the Zhivkov regime, Bulgarians protest the
failing successor government.*

Strikers in Sofia, Bulgaria, organize in front of the university.

Standing in a Sofia food line in subfreezing weather.

Searching for the cooking oil ration coupon in Sofia.

*Students Peter Todorov and Dimitar Dimitrov at their strike
headquarters in Sofia.*

*A family-filled apartment building in a good Sofia neighborhood
displays neglect that is typical in Bulgaria.*

trademark star and a demure-looking blonde either tying or untying her tuxedo tie. "Czech Auto Rent," reads the copy, "East beats West. Number One in CSFR." The brochure is in English and German and makes it clear that the cars rent for deutsche marks.

★   ★   ★

A continent away, one experience I had shows that Eastern Europe's current economic reality mocks political boundaries. I was reserving a Hertz car from California, trying to find the best price. I asked the clerk how much it would cost if I picked up the car in Munich. The price was 455 deutsche marks a week. "And what would it cost if I pick up the car in Belgrade?" Again the price was 455 deutsche marks. Finally, just to make sure I wasn't missing a better deal, I asked her about picking up the car in Prague. Her tone was exasperated. "Munich, Belgrade, Prague — the price is the same. It's all Germany."

Sure, she's just another geographically ignorant American. But the united Germany is well positioned to use the newly liberated Eastern Europe as its economic colony in much the same way that the United States makes use of Latin America. Germany sends just enough aid east to keep the economies there from collapsing. In return, Eastern Europe offers cheap vacations, a cheap source of labor, and a ready market for German products.

President Havel warned Czechoslovakians — and all of liberated Eastern Europe — against maintaining and developing prejudices against the Germans. On the fifty-first anniversary of the Nazi invasion of Czechoslovakia, Havel welcomed the West German president, Richard von Weizäcker, with the kind of moral message that makes Havel such a special politician. "To speak with disdain about the Germans is the same as to speak about the Vietnamese or the people of any nation," Havel said. "To condemn them only because they are Germans, to be afraid of them only because of that, is the same as to be anti-Semitic."

Václav Havel is a realist, too. He reminded the Germans, in the same speech, of the history that makes the world worried about Germany. "It is up to them to deprive Europe of fear," he said.

Time and again during his first year in office, Havel—the political prisoner turned president—made exquisite use of his position. One of the most impressive occasions was his speech to the United States Congress, when he asked, not for direct aid to Czechoslovakia, but American help for Gorbachev if it wanted to help preserve the improvements in Eastern Europe.

The Communist type of totalitarian system unintentionally gave Czechoslovakia something positive, Havel said in that speech to Congress, "a special capacity to look, from time to time, somewhat further than someone who has not undergone this bitter experience. A person who cannot move and live a somewhat normal life because he is pinned under a boulder has more time to think about his hopes than someone who is not trapped in this way."

★   ★   ★

All the rapid changes, even though most of them remain positive changes, are taking their toll. When we rented our flat in Prague the spring after the revolution, it was from a psychologist, Olga Sozanska, and she complained about her lack of free time. Her caseload keeps increasing, and she blames the new freedoms and their disturbing effects on people. "There is more anxiety now than in the past," she says. As hard as that may be to believe, Sozanska is in an ideal position to analyze the situation; she specializes in family counseling. "In the past, under the Communists," she says, "everyone knew what was sanctioned and what was not. Now suddenly people are free, and they are having to make decisions."

In her practice, Sozanska sees the revolution deeply affecting her clients' personal and professional lives. "It was an exciting time, and many of my married clients simply fell in love with other people," she says, explaining the growing number of extramarital affairs she and other psychologists are helping people deal with. The end of the Communist system means facing the competition of the marketplace, and that's disturbing society, too. "Capitalism is frightening," she says, "because suddenly the Communists, and all those people who got used to either not working or producing useless products, are told that they may lose their jobs."

Some of the people hardest hit psychologically were those who bought into the Communist system completely. "I had a nervous breakdown during the revolution," Václav Bervida, foreign editor of the Communist Party newspaper *Rude Pravo*, complained. "I simply could not function for two weeks. Before, the Communist Party was my god. Now I don't know what to believe in."

Even Bervida's newspaper deserted him. Before the first year of the revolution was out, it dropped "communist" from its masthead and started referring to itself as a "left-wing paper."

Revolutionaries like Jan Konvalinka could not comprehend the problems facing the psychologists. "A year ago I wouldn't have been able to imagine it," said Jan about his country as we celebrated the first anniversary of the revolution together at the Klub Novinar — the Press Club. "Now it is up to you, you can do what you want, I do not understand those who are depressed. Now I can do what I want." He was eating, drinking, smiling. "My friends are not depressed. I feel privileged to be here."

By November 1990, a year after the revolution, the red stars are down from the buildings around Wenceslas Square, and the American flags are up. George Bush's face grins out from official photographs stuck in store windows up and down the square in anticipation of his visit.

"Did you notice that the tape on all the pictures is the same?" asks Markos. "I wonder who stuck them up?" And he's right. On close inspection, it's clear that the photographs are not just a spontaneous show of affection. All of the pictures are secured with a piece of tape cut in the same unusual way and taped at exactly the same angle.

George Bush isn't the only invasion this weekend shortly before Christmas. Bus loads of American army families pour into Prague. The army organizes crystal-buying trips from Germany, advertised on American Forces Network radio stations.

The subdued sound of Czechs softly talking in the streets is broken into by piercing American voices.

"Is this the pizza place?"

"Yeah, this is the pizza place!"

The Americans drag suitcase carts to manage their hauls of crystal. Overweight, shoved into dumpy, unmatched pants and ski parkas, puffing on cigarettes, they contrast sharply with the elegant Prague natives.

Candles still burn; the flowers are still fresh with the pictures of revolutionary heroes at the top of the square as workers build the bullet-proof hut for Bush's speech. The mood is odd, with the overwhelming presence of the American president on the anniversary of the revolution. But one handmade banner in the square sums up the continuing feeling of the Czechoslovakians, a feeling that still transcends the problems. WE ARE HAPPY, it proclaims.

On the Charles Bridge, peddlers offer old Communist Party memorabilia. Lapel pins featuring Lenin go for just over a dollar. The air is still. In the quiet the murmur of the river and the footsteps create a real background for a street musician strumming a gentle "Home on the Range" on his Fisher's Mandolinette.

★   ★   ★

"It's much better when someone from your country comes, when we compare it with the Soviets, like Brezhnev," says Pavel Vavrik. He's a thirty-one-year-old metalworker from Moravia who is pushing his way through the crowd, trying to see more. "It's a great honor for our country because he's a personality from America." He talks about the revolution, about listening to the news on Radio Free Europe and Voice of America for encouragement. He reminisces about signing a petition for the release of Havel from prison, and then he surveys the jammed square and smiles, "I am very satisfied."

Havel makes a critical speech, "Today we are standing here somewhat embarrassed. We know very well what we still have to accomplish and the question springing up to mind is, Why do we find it so difficult?"

Bush uses the platform to push his Persian Gulf policy after offering a few platitudes, "There are no leaves on the trees, and yet it is Prague Spring. There are no flowers in bloom, yet it is Prague Spring. The calender says November 17, yet it is Prague Spring."

The crowd isn't impressed. The applause is just polite. "He's quite a showman," observes Peter Weiss, a sociologist and Civic Forum activist, after listening to Bush. "It's something unusual for us. Our Havel is much more rational." Weiss is wearing a baseball cap that says San Francisco on it. He's waving a Czechoslovak flag. "Maybe the message is that we are supposed to be partners now, that we are on the same side."

But Weiss has more on his mind than Bush's speech. He's back from a trip to America, and it wasn't what he expected.

"It was terrible in your country. Nobody drinking. Nobody smoking. Nobody making love. If the Communists had told the truth about the United States," he's laughing now, "no one in Czechoslovakia would want to go to the United States."

We're walking to a bar. "Communist propaganda presented America as an immoral place with sex and drugs. Nothing from this is true." He's laughing, but serious and surprised.

"It was not that land of freedom. On the beach they are dressed, even. I saw nobody in the United States embracing on the street. No girl and boy holding hands. No women without bra. I don't want to give the impression that I didn't like the United States. I liked it. The people were very friendly."

He paused and thought for a second. "It's not my picture of the United States that I created from the books of my youth. It was completely different."

At the bar we push through the crowd and offer the dirty glasses we grabbed from tables to the barkeep. Unless we bus the tables, there's nothing to drink from. As we settle into a corner, I see the Stars and Bars flying out in the street. Even after a day of watching Old Glory wave alongside the Czechoslovak flag, seeing the Confederate banner on the streets of Prague is a shock. The guy holding it is turned out in a black leather jacket and a white scarf.

He's happy to talk, clearly looking forward to a confrontation. "I am sympathizing with the South," he smiles in excellent English.

He's quick to introduce his profession ("I am a medical doctor") to try to give his speech some credibility. Forty years old, Doctor Igor Pinos and the cronies around him make clear the deep social problems facing liberated Eastern Europe.

"We have to learn to keep our identity as a white race. After the end of this century," he patiently explains, "white persons on this earth will make only ten percent of this earth. I think we must make some self-defense. Do you know lower Wenceslas Square, where Arabs and gypsies are . . ."

Most of the Prague black marketeers operate at the bottom end of the square, and most of them are Arab students. They not only change money illegally, cutting out the struggling official economy, they often stiff ignorant tourists. The scam is to swap out-of-date Czech crowns or virtually worthless Polish zlotys (the naive tourists usually can't differentiate between Czechoslovakian and Polish bills) for Western money. The poor tourist doesn't know he's been had until he tries to spend the money. A couple of blocks away is the main Prague gypsy bar, a headquarters for violent crime.

But Dr. Pinos is ready with a solution. "Before the war, during the Austro-Hungarian Empire, a person without a legitimate source of income was forced back to their birthplace." That's not all the doctor has in mind. "Without a little force we won't find a solution. The police must be reorganized and be much more professional. The police must come back to the street. The police are afraid. They have limited rights to use the force."

He looks up at his flag. "In my meaning, it is more than the American meaning." He can't quite understand why seeing the rebel flag is so disconcerting to me, and as a fellow from Philadelphia elbows his way through the crowd and also expresses irritation, the doctor muses, "Maybe I'm wrong, because I don't know exactly the meaning of this symbol in America. But in this country, it represents something very conservative and American."

★   ★   ★

The doctor may be waving his racist banner; Slovaks might be
circulating petitions against Hungarians; sophisticated Czechs
might complain about their more provincial Slovak partners; but
the differences facing Czechoslovakians, even combined with
their formidable ecological and financial challenges, don't carry
the doomsday quality of the conflicts facing other Eastern
European countries. There is a maturity and stamina evident in
the Czechoslovakian political mentality that suggests they won't
blow this chance at success.

Chapter Six

MAGYAR McDONALD'S

"Comrades, it's over!"
—Caption on Hungarian Democratic Forum campaign poster
over the back of a fat-necked Soviet soldier

IN HUNGARIAN SLANG, something that sounds almost exactly like, "See ya!" means hello. Hungarians meet each other in the street, say "See ya!" and start up a conversation. When they're finished, and it's time to say good-bye, the Hungarian slang they use is "Hallo!" Listening to Budapesters saying "See ya!" for hello and "Hallo!" for good-bye adds a twist of perpetual confusion for an American trying to figure what's happening along the Magyar reaches of the Danube.

My skills with the Hungarian language extend just a tad past "See ya" and "Hallo." I can count to ten and say, "How's Uncle Paul?" "Thank you for the dinner," and "Go to hell." It was a litany I used frequently to break the ice among Hungarians, and it was always well received with congenial laughs. The Hungarians employ a fun attitude toward life. There's plenty of wine and beer and rollicking gypsy music, cultural paraphernalia that made it easier for Hungarians to divert themselves as they plodded through their years of Communist deprivation.

On a snowy winter night in 1980, I made my way into Budapest on the train from Vienna. It was early evening, but the streets were already emptying as I walked from the station looking for a place to eat dinner. The falling snow muted the street noise and reduced the lacy neon store signs to glimmers.

I found an Italian restaurant, ate a long and leisurely dinner, drank Tokay, and talked with the waiter. He was in his early twenties and nervous about speaking the little bit of English he knew. But he kept returning to the table and telling me about his dream to move to Chicago. While he spoke, he looked around, checking to see who was watching. But he wanted the encounter more than he worried. I was the last customer that night, and finally he offered me a late sight-seeing trip through Budapest, if I waited until he finished with his duties.

We walked out into the now heavy snowstorm, and he put me in his old Lada. It took him a while to get the engine started and the windshield cleared, so to keep me amused, he popped a tape into the player: the Beatles. In a few minutes we were careening through the dark streets of Budapest, while the speakers blasted at full volume "Magical Mystery Tour."

He dropped me off at the second-class hotel that Ibusz, the state travel agency, had arranged for me back in Vienna. I invited him for breakfast the next morning and made my way up to my room past the bevy of prostitutes gracing the lobby.

Beautiful and pushy prostitutes were part of the scenery in Eastern European hotels, even the second-class hotels that catered to the Communist clientele and poorer Western travelers. Maria was one of several regulars at my hotel. She showed remarkable interest in an American fellow I was traveling with, so I saw a lot of her. The routine favored by Maria and her colleagues was brazen. She would come to work in the early evening, claiming her rights to the territory by walking behind the bar and dramatically depositing her purse on a shelf near the cash register for safekeeping. Then she would motion for a drink, cast her eyes around the bar sizing up potential customers, and nastily adjust her clothes before closing in on my friend. There was no secret about the business being conducted by Maria and her co-workers. Their clothing and makeup were just cheap and exaggerated enough that combined with their antics, they were like *Playboy* cartoon images of hookers. They seemed bizarrely out of place in the drab and formal lobby bar, the only luxury available.

My waiter friend never showed up for breakfast. By morning his paranoia had probably returned with enough force to overcome his interest in stories about Chicago. He didn't miss much at breakfast. The hotel was filled with Eastern European businessmen wearing brown suits that could have been stylish in the forties. We drank a watered-down Tang imitation and ignored the handful of Communist Party newspapers. The pictures showed the usual diet of a controlled press: head shots of the leaders, heroic production shots of farms and factories.

One of my cousins told me how he sifted information out of the controlled press all through the long, dark years. "We listened to the Voice of America for news," he explained. "But when VOA was jammed, we just read the denial page in the newspaper. That way we knew what was said and jammed on VOA and what stories to watch."

★ ★ ★

As the Iron Curtain rises, one danger Western observers face is the propensity for lumping together all the old Soviet Eastern European colonies. This is an easy trap to fall into, especially for Americans, because we are so far away and have long thought of this region as one unit: the Eastern bloc.

Over and over again a closer look shows that the opposite is the case. Each of the Eastern European countries is unique. Each faces a unique set of problems, and each is off on a very separate path to try to clean up the mess over forty years of authoritarian Communism has made of the region. In fact, those forty years of oppression and suppression are one of the few things the Soviet satellites do hold in common.

Life was usually so difficult throughout the Eastern bloc in the years following World War II that the individual nations had little opportunity to assert their own identity—or to lapse into the ethnic and nationalistic bickering that's produced war after war in Europe throughout history.

Now that people in countries like Hungary are again relatively free, they're free to fight with their neighbors again. One of the very few positive aspects of the Stalinist period is the peace the oppressors enforced.

Examples of bad relations with neighbors are too easy to find.

It's just a few hours from Vienna to Budapest. On the Austrian side of the border, huge supermarkets cater to Hungarians crossing over to buy goods still hard to get in Hungary. For those Hungarians with access to hard currency, buying in Austria saves money, too.

At the checkout counter in one of these markets, an enormous sign hangs near the cash register. It's impossible to miss, not only because of its size, but also because it is in the Hungarian language. All the other signs in the store are written in German. The sign demands that Hungarian shoppers — and only Hungarian shoppers — open their purses and bags for inspection to ensure that they're not stealing.

On the Transylvanian side of Hungary, the ethnic conflicts are much more serious. Transylvania now lies within Romanian national borders. But over the centuries this borderline moved back and forth often.

About two million ethnic Hungarians live inside what is now Romania. Once Ceauşescu and his dictatorship were overthrown, this Hungarian minority started lobbying hard for some basic civil rights, especially the right to study and use the Hungarian language. Political and cultural power for the Hungarian minority worries the ethnic Romanians living in Transylvania. During the revolution against Ceauşescu, the ethnic Hungarians and the Romanians managed to work together to overthrow their oppressor. But after he was removed, Romanians became whipped up with fear that the region could be returned to Hungary and the Romanians become the disadvantaged minority.

This conflict between the two nationalities led to a surge of street fighting just before the first post-Communist elections in Hungary in 1990. Romanians roamed the streets with clubs chanting, "Transylvania is Romanian!" looking for Hungarians to beat up. Other chants at the time were "Hungarians want to take back Transylvania!" and, ironically, "Death to Laszló Tokés!" Tokés is the pastor from Timişoara whose persecution inspired the Romanian revolution.

The Hungarians were vastly outnumbered during the street confrontations. At least six people died the week before the election, and hundreds were injured. The Romanian army moved in to enforce peace.

If the troubles weren't so pitifully tragic, the mindlessness of the confrontations would be laughable. Consider the crisis at Pharmacy Number 28 in Tirgu-Mures. That's the Romanian city where the violence was the worst in the spring of 1990 following the revolution. The official Hungarian News Agency issued a dispatch it called "The Pharmacy Affair" explaining the Hungarian side of the story. It quotes Ms. Emese Kormoczky, the deputy manager of the drugstore, denying that the store put up a sign in Hungarian reading, "This pharmacy only serves Hungarians."

"A report was carried in the daily *Adevault*," Kormoczky told the Hungarian agency. "The report makes it look as though from the moment we fixed the Hungarian name on the pharmacy, we only gave out medicine to ethnic Hungarians. This is a complete fabrication, lies, a falsification of the facts.

"True," the pharmacist continues, "we did make a sign with the word 'pharmacy' [*gyogyszertar*] written on it in Hungarian, but then we have a legal right to do this. But no way did we apply discrimination when dispensing medicine. For one thing, that wouldn't have been in keeping with the ethics of our profession."

Kormoczky told her sympathetic Hungarian audience that neighboring merchants incited passersby against Pharmacy Number 28, and that a mob then vandalized the place, all because of the Hungarian sign. She blamed false Romanian news reports for misinterpreting what the sign said.

Language represents much of the conflict. The Hungarians do not consider Tirgu-Mures to be Tirgu-Mures. To them it is Marosvásárhely. "We fight, we die, we don't give up Transylvania," chanted the Romanians. The Hungarian government insisted that its statement describing Transylvania as a "component of Hungary" was meant in an ethnic, not a political, context. "The Romanian language is obligatory throughout Romania!" responded the chanters.

The center-right party, the Hungarian Democratic Forum, used the trouble to gain votes on the basis of its nationalistic philosophy. Hungarian Jews worried that such nationalism would mean a rise in anti-Semitism.

Hungary appears to be well on its way to recovery from its Communist period. In many respects it is ahead of other Eastern European countries. But that means that Hungary is suffering hard from the economic troubles that come with the switch from Communism to a free market system. As government subsidies for needed consumer products disappear, prices rise dramatically. Western investment — when and if it comes — does not mean that the Hungarians (and other Eastern Europeans) get to enjoy a Western standard of living.

An example is the much publicized purchase of Tungsram by General Electric. GE took over the Hungarian government light bulb manufacturing company hoping to increase its share of the lucrative European light bulb market. GE executives were entranced by the low overhead at Tungsram; it produced the cheapest light bulbs of any European maker. Those appetizing production costs were easy to explain. The workers GE inherited earn an average of two or three thousand dollars a year.

It doesn't take much to realize that GE got itself a great deal. The harder question to answer is how the Tungsram workers can afford rising costs for food and shelter, let alone all the Western delicacies now gracing Hungarian grocery stores.

Budapest still looks a little ragged compared with its Danube sister city, Vienna. Vienna's opulent buildings glisten; full-length fur coats are everywhere. In Budapest, the wear and tear of the postwar years is apparent. Many buildings stand decaying, and damage from the war and from the 1956 revolution is still evident, like scars from machine gun bullets.

But compared with other Eastern bloc capitals, at first glance Budapest is a shining example of material success. The city's beautiful location helps. The Danube separates the hills of Buda from the downtown side of Pest. At night the bridges and the castles are lit up to rival Paris.

McDonald's is jammed day and night. The main shopping street is filled. The stores offer not just Hungarian folkloric embroidery for tourists, but also Western luxuries for Hungarians.

Even in the neighborhood groceries, there is no shortage of supplies. Markets are full of fresh fruits and vegetables. There's plenty of meat available. There are no long lines. Although in the state-run ABC grocery stores the lack of diversity is still an irritant, even those stores are developing a more varied stock. That sameness of available consumer goods was always one of the infuriating aspects of shopping in the Eastern bloc. No matter where you shopped in a country, the options were unchanged: the same hunks of the same cheeses, the same styles of bread, the same canned goods. Always exactly the same goods were available in all the stores, and rarely was there a choice within food groups. If you needed fruit, there was no need to decide what type of fruit. Whatever was in the cans the central planning office managed to find that week is what you brought home. I took home piles of Vegetexco pineapple juice and Mount Elephant Brand pineapple pieces while I was staying in Czechoslovakia.[1]

That's one of the reasons why returning from an extended stay in the East was always such an assault on the senses. The Wertheim is a department store in Berlin with an extensive supermarket in the basement. I remember wandering around the aisles with Sheila in a daze after returning from a long spell on the other side of the Iron Curtain. It was not just a shock to see the variety, it was amazing. So many different fruits and vegetables were there, and all of them perfect, not withered and rotting. The colors of the packaged goods were so vibrant and brilliant! The choices in the bakery section were endless. This

---

[1]A detailed reading of the labels meant a trip through the Communist world. The pineapple in Czechoslovakia was invariably imported by China National Cereals, Oils & Foodstuffs Import & Export Corporation, Guangxi, PRC.

supermarket experience, after coping with the limited repetition in the East, was dazzling. The Wertheim became a museum of food culture for us, and we lingered in the adventure, laughing and enjoying it, buying much more than we needed.

Probably the best-known German department store is the KaDeWe in Berlin, where the best of everything imaginable is available. There, on her first trip to the West, my friend Dagmar had the opposite consumer experience. Instead of pleasure, she felt dizzy from the affluence, revolted by the choices of toilet paper brands, the gourmet selection of expensive prepared foods. For her, the elegant KaDeWe was "an obscenity." It offended her to see so many unnecessary products sold and bought "when so many people elsewhere in the world do without the basic needs of life."

Dagmar is an exception. Most Eastern Europeans, denied basic consumer goods for so many years, let alone luxuries that are commonplace in Western Europe, jump at the chance to window-shop and wish they could scrape up enough money to buy the newly available merchandise. Who can blame them? Even those of us in the West who ridicule the conspicuous consumption culture do it from the vantage point of rejecting material goods that are readily available to us. Until Eastern Europeans get their chance at Barbies and Slurpies, Big Macs and Nintendo, and all the other junk the West offers, who can expect them to spurn it? And why shouldn't they get their chance to play with these toys that the West considers routine? American pop culture, crass as it may often be, is seductive, especially after it is forcibly denied.

Most Western tourists who stop off in Budapest just see the affluence there on Váci útca, the main drag of opulent shops and restaurants. That's where the McDonald's is located. Its glistening veneer makes even the hamburger joint look luscious. Only after you order a Tejturmix (chocolate, vanilla, or strawberry) and a Dupla Hamburger or a Dupla Sajtburger do you remember that though it might look rich, the taste is the same as under the Golden Arches worldwide.

McDonald's aside, Budapest is a luscious city, and that texture oozes onto Váci útca. Haute couture mixes with grocery stores offering paprika packaged in cute sacks for tourists and the unique Hungarian red salami. Street musicians and merchants jam the pedestrian zone, along with the money changers. Decrepit, shriveled peasant and gypsy women line up near the McDonald's holding up their hand-embroidered tablecloths, looking miserable and desperate, demanding and getting prices double those at stores away from Váci. Hipsters peddle sealed, but empty, cans labeled "the Last Breath of Communism" in a half dozen different languages.

Our Budapest apartment was right around the corner from the McDonald's. We rented two rooms from an Italian woman during the 1990 election campaign. Marriage brought her to Hungary, and she stayed even after it ended. The furniture was chic Italian-style from the mid-sixties. The walls were covered with paintings of our landlady, each done by a different artist. Every morning she would wake us with a knock and present us with espresso and steaming milk.

Like most folks who interact commercially with Westerners, she wanted to be paid in hard currency. In fact, we were broke when we rented the place and needed to get a cash advance with one of our credit cards. Electronic currency transfers had come to Hungary, but the cash came in forints, not dollars. Although the bill charged to our Visa card was ultimately in dollars, it was impossible to get the bank to give us an advance in dollars. The result was a loss to her, and to us. She wanted the dollars or deutsche marks badly. Paying in hard currency would have meant a heavy discount.

"Change money, change money," says the Lebanese guy. In the few blocks around the McDonald's, it is a battle just to get through the demanding money changers as they aggressively seek out foreigners carrying hard currency. Markos tries to dissuade the pushy Lebanese fellow by asking him to swap Soviet rubles into forints. Nobody wants rubles. It's a joke.

There are plenty of jokes to take the edge off life in Eastern Europe. Question: What do you call someone who speaks three languages? Answer: Trilingual. Question: What do you call someone who speaks two languages? Answer: Bilingual. And what do you call someone who speaks one language? An American.

Another joke: A fellow walks into a shop, looks around, and asks, "Is there no bread here?" "No," answers the clerk, "this is a butcher shop; there's no meat here. There's no bread across the street at the bakery."

The Lebanese money changer is living in Budapest with his Hungarian wife because Beirut became too dangerous for him. "Budapest is so quiet," he jokes; "I can't sleep without bombs going off." But then he seriously complains, "Budapest is so boring; nothing happens here." He waves at Váci útca and dismisses it, "This is not Budapest."

He's correct. The few blocks of luxury do not represent the struggle life continues to be for most Hungarians as the country makes its way toward capitalism. Two wage earners in a family, or moonlighting workers, or just plain doing without the basics of modern society are more common aspects of life in Hungary than frittering away an afternoon over Viennese coffee and pastries after shopping at the Benetton and Adidas stores.

But even on this trendy street, the legacies of the failed Communist economy remain. People are used to shortages, used to products being unavailable, used to making do without enough. A prime example came when the batteries in my Fuji camera gave out. Now, this camera takes a special lithium battery that is an odd size and unique to the camera. I checked a couple of the fancy camera stores without luck. But one of the shops did stock a lithium battery of the voltage my camera needed. It would not fit in the slot that takes the two batteries designed for my camera, but the clerk had a practical suggestion. Years of experience with the central planning system had taught her that it was unlikely she would be able to find, order, and get the correct batteries delivered. In fact, from her vantage point, she considered it quite lucky that she had a battery that was electrically compatible with my camera. She recommended that I just wire this wrong battery into the camera and secure it somehow to the outside of the case, or try to cut the battery so that it would fit into the compartment. This was a suggestion that would never come from a camera store just a few hours up the Danube in Vienna, on the other side of the rising Iron Curtain. In Vienna the appropriate battery would be quickly ordered. In Budapest we learn how to make do.

*   *   *

After the Soviet Union smashed the 1956 revolution, Hungarians accepted the political power of the Soviets and went about working around that reality to improve their standard of living. It was called goulash Communism, a mix of controlled centrally planned and market economies. Despite continued government ownership of large factories and businesses, local management was encouraged to run competitive operations based on market needs. Profit making was encouraged. Small private shops were allowed to open, and they prospered. But the freedom Hungarians enjoyed from 1987 on to travel abroad accelerated the exodus of money from the country. Already, much of Hungary's improved living standard was being financed with money borrowed from the West that the government poured into the artificially supported economy. Now that they were traveling abroad, Hungarians started spending outside the country much of the little money that they were accumulating. That drained the national economy further, making it harder for poorer Hungarians to earn enough money to keep up with increasing prices. One result is that although goods are available, most Hungarians don't have the money to buy a McDonald's Dupla Sajtburger or pork steaks very often.

In fact, as the Iron Curtain rose, Hungary was filling with the social problems so prevalent in the West during the latter half of the twentieth century and almost unknown in the old Eastern bloc: skyrocketing inflation, unemployment, homelessness, and a declining standard of living.

The Hungarian forint was still not a convertible currency. When Hungarians want to travel, or buy something not available in Hungary, they must earn Western money. That usually means exchanging money on the black market or selling goods and services for Western currency.

This makes Hungary a bargain for Westerners and a frustration for Hungarians trying to interact with the world economy.

* * *

Hungarians responded to Khrushchev's denunciation of Stalin in 1956 by expecting positive change. They replaced their own Stalinist leader with a reformist, Imre Nagy. Nagy announced Hungarian neutrality, and the Soviets reacted by invading Hungary. The worst of the fighting lasted just a week, as the tanks crushed the revolt. Nagy was executed. A few hundred thousand Hungarians left the country.

Those who stayed forged the goulash compromise, accepting the power of the tanks and the overall authority of the Soviet Union, while working out economic devices to improve their standard of living. János Kádár, who found it easy to switch from Nagy's team to the Soviet side once their troops were in control, took over the government. Slowly, as living conditions improved, political restrictions lessened. When Hungarians were allowed free travel in 1987, there was no wholesale exodus of people from the country.

In 1989, Hungarians made their move to get rid of their Communist government. By contrast with the violent overthrow that was to come a few months later across the border in Romania, a series of events caused the Communists to quietly succumb.

The 1989 Hungarian revolution started March 15, perfect for challenging the Communists because it is a date honored by most Hungarians. On March 15, 1848, Hungarian reformers, led by the poet Sándor Petöfi, made twelve basic demands during their successful and bloodless revolution. From a free press and abolition of censorship to civil and religious equality, from jury trials and freedom for political prisoners to unity with Transylvania, the twelve demands continue to be rallying points for Hungarians.

Consequently, the Communist rulers found it impossible to avoid giving official sanction to the cross section of Hungarians who called for a huge street demonstration for March 15, 1989. Organizers skillfully called it a celebration, not a demonstration. The day was declared a national holiday for the first time in Hungarian history. Opposition politicians co-opted the bland official program arranged by the Communists and instead gave speeches reasserting the ideals of the 1848 revolution.

In response, the Communists, the Hungarian Socialist Workers' Party, issued a list of points of their own, sixteen of them for 1989. The list showed how out of touch with reality the old rulers were. While opposition politicians were drawing crowds by talking change, the exclamation points and the empty rhetoric on the HSWP list looked like the work of desperation:

1. March 15 belongs to the entire nation!

2. Let there be peace, freedom and consensus!

3. National unity — Yes; division — No!

4. Democratic socialism!

5. A free, democratic, socialist society!

6. If there is no democracy, there is no socialism!

7. A democratic multi-party system!

8. Greater independence to villages and cities!

9. Local independence, austere budget!

10. Comprehensive wages reform, the lawful recognition of the right to strike!

11. The HSWP fights for the ensurance of individual and collective rights of the Hungarians living in a minority!

12. Restructuring is needed not only in the economy!

13. Better tax system, proportionate bearing of public burdens!

14. Cheaper state, less bureaucracy!

15. Autonomy, academic freedom in higher education!

16. Our grandchildren also want to see our natural resources![2]

It was number 7 in that otherwise hollow list that the country paid attention to; it was the key to getting rid of the Communists. The next step came three months later when the streets of Budapest filled again for the official funeral of Imre Nagy, a ceremony denied him and the rest of the country after he was hanged in 1958. Just weeks later, János Kádár, the man who turned on Nagy and then led Hungary—filled with Soviet troops—to limited freedom and prosperity, died.

The rest of the Communist party accepted defeat, working with the opposition to set up rules for elections. Hungarian voters appreciated their flexibility, but nevertheless seized the opportunity to get rid of the Communists and not give them a second chance.

In the first free election since the Communists took control of the government in 1947, the old Communists, split into two new parties, took only 10 percent of the vote—enough to participate in the parliament. But it was a distant third place, clearly a loss.

As it was in East Germany, the break with the past is complete. The newspaper *Daily News* announced in its special election-results edition, "Tears were scarcely shed as Hungary switched political systems practically overnight."

But few Hungarians are expecting the new system to mean overnight changes in their personal lives. One Budapest man told me he considers the election a long step toward Europe. We talked at a schoolhouse far from the glitter of Budapest's tourist strip. This was a dirty district of crumbling apartment houses

---

[2]Along with the HSWP sixteen points, the detailed platforms of the twelve new, reorganized, and resurrected political parties that managed to qualify for the March 25, 1990, Hungarian national election were printed in an election special of the Hungarian News Agency newspaper *Daily News* and distributed the week before the election.

and factories; traffic raced by, headed for the main highway to Szeged. There was no school the day we met; the building had been commandeered for use as a polling station, and Kamuthy Balász was spending the day as an enthusiastic election worker.

After growing up in Communist Hungary, he had yet to shake his skepticism, even though he was involved in the changing system. He was worried that somehow the Communists would fix the results and steal yet another election.

"Maybe because now the Communists have the power, they do this election, and maybe they can do something with this election," is how he put it. He studied over the problem, "It is possible, but I think it will be okay. The Communists can do something; I'm a little worried because I don't know the system of control. I hope everything will be okay. I think, but I'm not sure."

Balász was kept busy. Most of the voters had no idea how to deal with the opportunity to select from a varied list of parties and candidates. But Hungary's election would have been complicated for any voter, no matter how experienced. A dozen different parties fielded candidates for the first balloting.

"Maybe after this election," he said, "we will have a democratic government. It is a historic occasion for Hungary."

A steady stream of voters made their way into the polling station. They patiently waited in line, quietly. The mood was sober, a reflection of the importance of the event. But there was quiet chatting among the voters; they seemed content, happy to be participating.

First they showed their national identity cards and then their voter registration slips. The information was checked against a master list. Then the voters made their way past a light blue curtain into the voting booth, marked their ballots, slipped them into special envelopes, and dropped them into the ballot box, a box secured with tape in the red, white, and green Hungarian national colors.

"I think my life won't change very much," Balász said about the election results, "but my son and daughter will live in a free country. I don't think it will change very much in a month," he said, musing that perhaps in ten or fifteen years he can expect to have a job, a flat, clothes for his children, and the opportunity to eat meat every day if he wishes.

★   ★   ★

One of my cousins is recommending that his daughter change her last name so that she doesn't need to worry about suffering from anti-Semitic discrimination at her job. She dismisses his concern. But he remembers that his brother was shot by the fascists during World War II and dumped into the Danube.

"I've always been with the left," he told me, explaining why he was voting for the reformed Communists in the election. "The Communists were established after the war by four Jews who committed terrible crimes against the people and the nation."

We were driving him back to his house after dinner. It's a concrete block apartment building, far from the bustling center of Budapest. The rooms are tiny; there is no elevator. But the apartment is his, and its egalitarian size and style fits with his philosophy.

"The Communists committed these terrible crimes," he was telling me in the car in response to my request that he try to explain the resurgence of prejudice against Jews, "and they were Jews. Now the opposition is using that as an opportunity to create new anti-Semitism to galvanize support."

Watch for the codes, he cautioned. "When Christian is in a party name, it is a code word for anti-Semitism; it is not Christian in the correct sense of the word."

So he voted for the new Socialist Party. He's convinced it's made up of the good guys, those politicians who were in the old ruling Communist Party and worked to institute reforms over the last twenty years.

His daughter does not intend to change her surname, but she doesn't dismiss her father's worries. She too is convinced that religious discrimination is returning. But she's not worried for her safety, just her future. The kind of anti-Semitism she's finding is much more subtle than the bullets that sent her uncle into the Danube. She sees Jewish colleagues passed over for promotion at the workplace.

Her immediate concern continues to be catching up with the rest of the world. "We've wasted forty years," she said to me softly in a sad voice that only sounds sadder with the lilting, musical Hungarian accent. There is a softness built into the intonations of Hungarian that make it impossible to sound shrill or angry. The newscasts on the radio take on an imploring tone; normal conversation — doing business in a store, for example — transmits a kind of warmth. So her succinct conclusion, "We've wasted forty years," comes across without anger or need for revenge but with a sad acceptance of unnecessary loss.

The Hungarian ambassador to the United States, Peter Zwack, responded to charges of growing anti-Semitism with an outraged letter to the *New York Times*. "Hungary today," wrote Zwack, "is a society of laws that protect and guarantee civil liberties. Under the law, perpetrators of anti-Semitic acts are punished. These ugly and deplorable incidents are not tolerated by the government of Prime Minister Jozef Antall. However, legal action cannot in itself eradicate covert and pernicious forms of anti-Semitism, as Western democracies know only too well."

★   ★   ★

The neon bar sign glows blue with the words *Drink Bar* in English off in the corner of the lobby of the hotel in Szeged, nestled in eastern Hungary near the Romanian border. Back when the opening of the Iron Curtain and the overthrow of East bloc Communism was no more than a fantasy, this part of Hungary was witnessing the breakdown of civilization in Romania. Thousands and thousands of Romanians risked arrest and torment by the Ceauşescu dictatorship to make their way across the border and ask for political asylum in Hungary. Many of the refugees were ethnic Hungarians, running from prejudice in addition to economic difficulties. But others were ethnic Romanians, seeking a better life in the more open environment of changing Communist Hungary than they could hope to find at home.

We shared a beer with the hotel manager. He had just offered us a nice price for the room — twelve dollars each in the first-class hotel, complete with direct dial telephones and American and British English-language TV coming in on satellite.

"The government is changed." Jánes Boros was high-strung and animated, moving his arms as he talked, looking at us intently. He was equipped with a healthy mustache and a bag with essentials hung across his chest. We were chatting several months after the election, after the violence against ethnic Hungarians in Transylvania. We were on our way to Romania, and he was urging us to be wary and cautious, telling me I look Hungarian.

"We have democracy," Boros told us, "but the people are the same." It was the same message Grzegorz kept repeating in Poland — only from Grzegorz it came out, "The same crooks are still in charge."

A fellow walks toward us from the bar. "A gypsy child," says Boros. American flag patches are sewn on the guy's jacket. He picks us out as Americans and sticks out his hand, demanding in a thick Hungarian accent, "Come on! Gimme five!" Then he asks where we are from.

"California."

"Yeah, yeah!" he's pleased. "This is America," he proudly points to the flag on his jacket, and then, seemingly out of English, adds a jaunty "See you later," snaps his fingers, and walks out of the bar like a bad combination of James Dean, Marlon Brando, and John Wayne.

"Hungary is the end of Europe," Boros is talking about Romania again. "There," he gestures east, toward the border, "it's not the same; it's another civilization. I cannot understand why there is this problem against the Hungarians."

Chapter Seven

UNREALITY IN ROMANIA

"Corn, I don't believe it's my corn."

— Caption for a front-page photograph
in a 1990 Timişoara newspaper,
showing a pair of hands cradling corn
after forty-five years of deprivation

THE CLOCK SLIPS back at the Romanian border. It is late 1990, almost winter, almost a year after the revolution that overthrew Ceauşescu. But many of the irritations and oddities that accompanied border crossings along the Iron Curtain before it rose are still in place.

The crossing is slow. A line of cars sits, engines off, drivers and passengers wandering around looking at the meager pickings available at the border kiosk: cigarettes and candy. The entrance visa still costs thirty U.S. dollars, even though border fees were dumped months before by the other liberated Eastern bloc countries.

Inside the concrete customs building, the lighting is dim. The lobby is stacked full of tires, and the smell of rubber is strong. One old, dumpy customs woman stands with the tires. There's no other sign of business in the building, no explanation for the tire warehouse.

After a routine passport check, there is a customs inspection. The chief inspector is wearing jeans, a civilian jacket — like a ski parka — dark glasses, and a beard. He looks as though he's in his thirties.

"Do you have any guns?"

"No."

". . . or roses?" He laughs and asks, "Do you know the band Guns 'n' Roses?"

"Yes," I answer tentatively. "Do you like them?"

He smiles his approval of the band. After a few days in post-Ceauşescu Romania it becomes understandable how a band that peddles intolerance would be a hit there.

But we're still not through the gate, not yet in the country. Markos offers the guard a package of Kents as he's searching the car. We had come equipped with plenty of Kents; Romanians are famous for loving them. That brand, for some inexplicable reason, is the most sought after; Kents are used as second currency. But a border guard can afford to be fussy. He dismisses the offered cigarettes with disdain and reverse snobbery.

"I only smoke Camels."

The paperwork continues, delayed and slow. Markos is equipped with a valid visa, but the passport checker refuses to accept it. He is forced back to the visa hut to get another thirty-dollar stamp. While he's buying the new visa, the guard that refused to accept his valid old one is kissing the visa lady on the back of the neck. It's hard to imagine that they won't be splitting that extra thirty dollars when their shift ends.

The covered drive through the inspection zone is decorated with faded tourist signs that suffer from poor color reproduction—like bad Technicolor—advertising hotels and campgrounds. The result is a failed attempt to intrigue visitors with Romania as an appealing ski resort or health spa destination. Instead, these deteriorating posters work as statements of reality, making it clear that ahead lies a failed system, a system that cannot even promote itself without drawing attention to internal decay.

The last passport check comes at a dirty window marked: SKON RO L. It used to say PASSKONTROLL; the plastic letters have dropped off, and no one cares enough to replace them. Above the SKON RO L sign is a rusting fluorescent light fixture with no tube in it and no evidence of recent use. Finally, the guard lifts the red-and-white metal gate, and we're in Romania, driving toward Arad.

This main highway is two lanes. Cars and trucks share the road with horse-drawn cargo wagons. Sheepherders in full-length sheepskin coats make their way alongside the road with their flocks.

On the outskirts of Arad is the first gas station, with a long line of decaying East bloc cars waiting. I get out to take a look and a picture as a kid approaches with a handful of tickets.

"Buy gas coupons? Change money?"

I shake my head and start to snap the camera at the line. He stops me.

"No photo. Police problem."

The black market in money and gas is wide open, but documenting the way of life here is dangerous. A few blocks farther on, a track gang is fixing the railroad. The work is being done with hand tools. Many of the laborers are old women: chubby, bundled up against the cold, their heads wrapped in babushkas.

On the main drag in Arad, the money changers work like vultures around the fanciest hotel, the Astoria. They jump at us, "I'll make a deal for you!" The crumbling economy supports an active black market. Officially, a dollar buys thirty-five lei, the bills worn almost to tissue paper from long use. But black, a dollar can bring one hundred ten lei.

The question remains — aside from the risk of arrest, or the likelihood that the money changer is a crook and passes on worthless obsolete bills — what is there to buy with bargain lei? Hotel stays require payment with money exchanged at the official rate, the hotel cashiers check for a money exchange receipt. Restaurants are dirt cheap at any rate. There is not much else for sale, let alone much of interest to take home. Just as in most of the old Communist world, the new opportunities to do business are tempered by the reality that there is actually very little to bother taking West.

Inside the Astoria, the lobby is dark and cold, the bar crowded with noisy drinkers. Pieces of the wall are crumbling off; paint is faded and patched. Five back-lit digital clocks adorn the wall offering the time in New York, London, Bucharest, Moscow, and Tokyo. Lights are burned out in all but Bucharest, and it tells the wrong time.

The porter–concierge–security man looks like one of the Three Stooges. His stocky body is stuffed into a tight, mismatched pinstriped suit: brown-striped pants, a blue-striped jacket, a striped shirt, and a neatly knotted striped tie. He smiles under his beret.

A few doors down from the Astoria, graffiti on a wall—in English—sums up much of what we're about to encounter: "Fuck the Front."

"Now it's a democracy in Romania, you can do what you want!" The seventy-year-old woman is exuberant about the changes she's seen in the last year—changes she never expected to see: an apparently vibrant press, the opportunity to travel, some hope for the future. Reference to the changes shows up in almost every sentence she speaks, even when she is just giving directions, "Turn right at the big building. It used to be a party building; now it is the city hall!"

The official literature has yet to catch up with the political changes. The Arad County Tourist Office offers a brochure that proclaims, "It is in the years of socialist construction that Arad has known unprecedented development, particularly after the year 1965, since comrade Nicolae Ceauşescu, the first president of socialist Romania, has been at the helm of the party and Romanian state."[1]

The lies of the leftover propaganda are absurd. A booklet called "The Charming Romanian Folk Art and Folklore" asserts, "Owing to historical conditions in some areas of the country, coinhabiting nationalities such as Hungarians, Germans, and others have lived for centuries in unity and brotherliness alongside Romanians; this coexistence is reflected in the spiritual life and creation, in terms of the syncretism of this creation

---

[1]From the booklet "Arad County," published by the Oficiul Judetean Arad in 1987 and still available in late 1990 through the tourist office at its Hotel Astoria address: Bd. Republicii 79–81, Arad.

and of the mutual influences involved in it."[2] While the tourist office was busy passing out this foolishness, the ethnic Hungarians in Romania were being attacked by their fraternal ethnic Romanians, and the ethnic Germans in Romania were busy arranging emigration to the good life in Germany.

★ ★ ★

Lines form suddenly in Arad, out of nowhere, when goods show up. There's a long line in the bitter cold outside a butcher shop as a truck full of sausage is unloaded. Shelves in a hardware store are jammed, but with only a handful of different items. One style of oil lamp, one style of knife and one style of brush fill the store. A dollar at the official rate buys one of the oil lamps, complete with chimney and reflector.

Black-and-white photographs of brides and grooms decorate the window of a photography studio. The lack of color pictures in the show window adds to the toned-down mood of the business district compared with the flash available just a few miles across the border in Hungary.

Beggars work the street to the marketplace, sitting on the pavement in the freezing cold, dirty. The open-air market is alive with shoppers after fresh fruit and vegetables and animals. Piles of deep red, freshly ground paprika dust are offered by babushka-covered vendors. Locally produced folk music for sale on cassettes is blaring from a boom box; it sounds Turkish. Beat cops mix lazily through the market, stopping at one table and openly picking up a plastic bag full of cigarettes — smugly, it seems, taking their bribe.

A crumbling building, with soft corners that make it appear more Oriental than European, faces the marketplace; an attached satellite dish calls attention to the twentieth century.

---

[2]The Romanian propagandists dug deep into their dictionaries to find *syncretism*. It comes from the Greek, combining *union* and *Cretan*, and means the attempts at combining or reconciling different beliefs, as Cretan villages managed to do with their various forms of the Greek language. This 1989· booklet originated at the Ministry of Tourism, National Tourist Office, 7 Magheru Blvd., 70161 Bucharest.

Crates of Pepsi bottles are stacked on a street corner for sale, filled with a variety of lemonade-colored sodas, homemade and home-bottled. The Romanian-language signs are recognizable. Old women come out of Alimentara Produse din Carne with sheets of lard. Gypsies with flats of salvaged broken eggs make their way through the crowds of shoppers. The uniform of these women: short leather jackets, brilliant and clashing colored skirts, wild eyes. The gypsy men wear dumpy suits.

A little kid, maybe ten, looks into the window of the closed dollar shop at the unavailable chocolate. Not only is the store closed, he cannot shop there with whatever lei he might have; it is a government hard currency shop, offering luxuries and drawing whatever hard currency it can out of the economy and passing foreigners. The boy asks for dollars so he can buy chocolate when the store opens, and he asks for a push to get his homemade motorcycle going. It is just an engine mounted on a reinforced bicycle frame with pounded-out sheet metal for fenders. It sputters and starts, and off he goes with a lopsided heading; the wheels and frame are not aligned.

In the main square in Timişoara, flowers and pine boughs are piled around pictures of martyrs from the 1989 revolution. A typed poem, protected from the weather by a sheet of plastic, rests on the memorial. One sad-looking black-and-white photograph in an old wooden frame stands out among the heroes:

Erou al Revolutiei
Hategan Petru
11.06.43–17.12.89

Hero Hategan was killed on the second day of the revolution. On the post–World War II buildings near the memorial, pockmarks from automatic weapons fire remain. The paths of the bullets are clear, showing which windows and balconies were targets. The spray paint on the walls is a reminder that the revolution is not over: FSN = PCR, the National Salvation Front equals Ceauşescu's Communist Party.

December in Romania means it's dark and cold by late afternoon. Lines for the grocery stores extend into the streets. In the freezing dark, flats of fresh eggs are for sale from impromptu open-air markets. The waiting is patient. A dozen different political tabloids are available from newsstands: *Opinia, Zigzag, Indiscret, Democratia, Independentul,* their titles suggesting a newly freed press.

But in its 1990 year-end report on world press freedom, the International Press Institute announced, "One of the saddest sights in the world media scene was that of Romania slipping back into some of the same forms of repression as those used against the press during the horrendous dictatorship of Nicolae Ceauşescu. The government of the National Salvation Front is treating the opposition as traitors and using television as a propaganda tool. Once again, the press has been forbidden to speak the truth."

The IPI report goes on to detail the abuse. "Pro-government newspapers pour out venom against critics. *Azi,* the official newspaper of the National Salvation Front, is a thug's guidebook. In one issue, it published the names, addresses, and telephone numbers of two journalists who had written articles critical of the front. That was one way pro-government miners knew how to pick their targets in June when they assaulted members of the opposition."

"Romania," concluded the IPI report sadly, "cannot boast a single genuinely independent newspaper or publisher, because all printing facilities are government controlled. Newspapers have become very cautious for fear of losing their right to publish at all."

★   ★   ★

In the Timişoara cold, men gather in the main square. The informal meetings are a nightly tradition since the revolution, to huddle and talk football and politics. The number-one complaint is not enough work, number two is that the government is still Communist.

"Exists a little liberty," explains one of the men in halting English, "but not enough money." His English is plenty good enough to make his opinion clear, "Better now liberty. A little liberty is better. But we want both."

What is next?

"I don't know, perhaps another revolution, another government, a coalition government with liberals, not FSN, but pluralists . . ."

Another violent revolution?

The response is a loud chorus of NO, NO, NO! "We'll wait and vote in a new government." The men smoke cigarettes, anxious to talk.

"People are losing jobs. Prices are going up. People are afraid maybe we'll be more poor."

Marius Jiranu is twenty-nine, a locksmith with ten years' experience and no work. He's come to Timaşoara from his village looking for work and thinks he'll be forced to search outside Romania. "The only people who are going to stay here are the Communists. I don't know what is going to happen. I have nowhere to go. It is impossible to get a visa into another country except to do contract work in South Africa." Even that is hard to arrange. The company coordinating the job placement is in Austria, and virtually no visas are available for Romanians to get to Vienna. Working in South Africa is not a moral question for Jiranu and his buddies, "We think there is more democracy there than in Romania."

"It is very hard to live in Romania," comes from Adrian Barbu, a twenty-two-year-old lathe operator. "There is nothing to eat in the shops, and now the price is going to go up. A new Dacia car is two hundred twenty thousand lei." Barbu calculates it would take him twenty to thirty years to make that much money.

"If I want to eat something, I no buy this car. This is the situation."

We want the world to help us, the men say in chorus again, not with money but with work.

"I don't like this Communist government, this Communist leader," complains Jiranu about Ceauşescu's successor, Ion Iliescu.

"Here in Romania," echoes Barbu, "in one year nothing happened. I hope something will happen. Ion Iliescu is from Moscow driven."

*   *   *

What did happen for Christmas in 1989 was an uprising inspired by first the East Germans breaking through the Berlin Wall and then the Czechoslovakians overthrowing their Communist dictatorship. The ethnic Hungarian pastor Laszló Tokés was at home. He was a troublemaker to the Ceauşescu government, frequently speaking out against abuses to human rights, and particularly the rights of ethnic Hungarians living in Transylvania. At the time, one of Ceauşescu's more ambitious and devious schemes was gathering momentum. The "helmsman who guides," as Ceauşescu ordered himself described, decreed that many farming villages, including ethnic Hungarian villages, villages dating back hundreds of years, were to be razed. They were to be replaced with the supposedly more efficient huge apartment blocks that desecrate so much of Eastern Europe.

The plan, identified by the newspeak label "systemization," was well publicized in Western Europe, where appalled activists were trying to organize opposition to the destruction and appealed to Ceauşescu to stop the cultural massacre. The protests were ignored by the "most eminent personality of international political and scientific life." The memorials to systemization are apartment buildings towering out of farmland.

Laszló Tokés was one of the few people inside Romania who dared to publicly work against the village relocation programs. In December 1989, word spread through Timişoara that Tokés was going to be removed, to stop his interference with progress. Brave parishioners circled his home to protect him. Shots were fired by the Securitate to disperse the crowd.

Instead, the shooting stimulated more antigovernment demonstrations. Within a few hours, the National Salvation Front took over the television studios and transmitters. Ceauşescu was out of the country at the time. Finally he returned and spoke to a crowd now filling Bucharest streets. He was jeered. The jeering, one of the first public attacks on Ceauşescu ever, was broadcast on nationwide TV. Then, suddenly, the screen went black. But the audio continued with a sound never before broadcast in Romania, the sound of the people jeering Ceauşescu. Demonstrations continued and turned into street fighting when the army and the Securitate attacked the crowds.

Then the army sided with the demonstrators against the secret police. After days of bloody street fighting, Ceauşescu and his supporters — many of them members of his family — were defeated. Ceauşescu himself ran, but he was caught in hours, tried, and immediately executed. The National Front, so quickly in place governing the country, organized as a political party and won the 1990 election.

The lingering question is, Was this a revolution or a palace coup? Much of the Front is made up of old Ceauşescu cronies, adding to the theory widely held in Romania that whatever popular revolution started in Timişoara was co-opted by insiders who wanted to get rid of Ceauşescu and his family reign, but not the ruling techniques and power of the Communist Party organization with which they were so closely affiliated.

★   ★   ★

As they did in the other countries occupied by the Soviet Army and left behind the Iron Curtain after World War II, Communists manipulated the electoral process to secure control of the Romanian government. Royalty was replaced by apparatchiks. In her book *Europe,* Flora Lewis describes a scene from that period that epitomizes the bizarre contrasts the Communists brought to the world scene as they took power:

> From the outside the most visible member of the leadership was Ana Pauker, a grim-faced, lumpy woman who kept her iron-gray hair in an awkward bob and wore ill-fitting mannish suits. There was no more telling image of what was happening in Romania than her arrival on an official visit to Warsaw in 1947. She went by train — air service was still uncertain — and used one of the luxurious old Orient Express specials, newly painted and polished. The Warsaw station had been totally destroyed in the war, made into a crater of twisted tracks. So Mrs. Pauker's train pulled up in an open clearing just outside the city, where the Polish

dignitaries lined up to greet her. The contrast between her and her escort was even greater than that between the elegant cars and the devastation. At each window as the train slowed to a stop were the men of her honor guard, wearing extravagant red and blue uniforms with operetta decorations. Some were obviously corseted, their cheeks and lips rouged, their moustaches waxed and twirled. Then came Ana Pauker. She clomped to the ground, eyes steely and lips sternly set. She made no concessions. The men around her were nothing more than Romania's vanishing past.

By the time Ceauşescu took over the government in 1965, Romania already was distancing itself from Moscow. Romanian troops, for example, did not join the rest of the Warsaw Pact invading Czechoslovakia in 1968 to force an end to the Prague Spring reforms. But at home, Ceauşescu made life miserable for Romanians. Like other Eastern bloc Communists, his government restricted travel and eliminated intellectual freedoms. In addition, he pursued a relentless policy of ridding Romania of foreign debt and foreign dependence. The result, when combined with inefficient factories and farms, was an inadequate supply of poor-quality consumer goods, not enough food, and not enough energy.

Concern about Ceauşescu Communists in the National Salvation Front prompted the Timişoara Proclamation. Signed by Timişoara revolutionary leaders and groups, and read to a rally in Timişoara's Opera Square a few months after the 1989 revolution, the proclamation pleads to keep Communists out of the political process until there is an opportunity to build an alternative society. "Timişoara started the revolution against the communist regime and its whole apparatus," reads point 7, "not to see the political ascent of a group of anti-Ceauşescu dissidents. Their presence at the head of the country makes it seem that the heroes of Timişoara died in vain."

But the leader of the National Front and president of Romania, Ion Iliescu, dismisses street demonstrations against his government, insisting in a speech to the parliament that those working against the Front are engaged in a "systematic

attempt to distort the intentions of the revolution to further
their own interests."

*   *   *

We encounter one of the signers of the Timişoara Proclamation
that night in the main square. Beaten by remnants of the
Securitate for his trouble, he's still at work; this night he's hoarse
from yelling, "Down with the Communists!" at a rally the
evening before. Despite his sore throat he's smoking a cigarette
and offers the pack.

"I don't smoke," I say and add the line that seems to work as
an explanation all over Eastern Europe, where declining a cigarette creates confusion among people who all seem to smoke
perpetually. "I'm from California."

"Do you know why you don't smoke?" the hoarse Timişoara
revolutionary asks me.

"Because it's bad for you," I venture, knowing it's not the
answer he's looking for.

"You're from California," he explains. "You don't smoke
because you have nothing to worry about. We smoke because
we worry."

*   *   *

Posted on the doorway of a building is a handwritten sign
announcing a meeting of the "Partidul Radical Transnational,
Transpartinic, Nonviolent." Inside a hall in the building a few
dozen Romanians are gathered in the dim light, wrapped
against the cold in their winter coats and hats. It's been a year
since the revolution. There still is not enough light or heat in
Romania. The meeting is an organizing session called by the
Radical Party, most famous for its member in the Italian Parliament, the blue-movie star Ilona Stalling. The Hungarian-born
Stalling goes by the name Cicciolina in Italy, and livens up the
parliament by periodically taking off her clothes or offering to
satisfy Saddam Hussein's aggressive urges by becoming his love
slave.

There's no sign of such frivolity at the Timişoara meeting,
where a Belgian party member, Olivier Dupuis, is presiding. He
sees no problem with coming to Romania, as a Belgian, and

trying to spread his politics. "I think I am at home in Romania," he says, "and they can be at home in Belgium. We work together." He calls it trans-European radical organizing. Then he gets to work. The big problem facing Romania, he says, is the human rights problem. "The problem of the Hungarians is perhaps not the worst. Perhaps it is the gypsies because they are for the moment less organized." But his audience is not doing much talking. "I think there is confusion after forty years of totalitarianism" is how he explains the lack of response. "People are a bit afraid to discuss." Perhaps the crowd is just happy for some free entertainment inside, out of the bitter chill on the streets.

★   ★   ★

It is getting late and colder. One of the men in the crowd out in the square offers us a place to stay at his apartment. He is Krísti Balan, in Timişoara staying with his cousins while he looks for work. He can't find a job in his native Moldavia on the other side of Romania. We insist on treating him to dinner and ask him to pick the place to eat.

We follow Krísti down an extremely dark street. The few street lights are dim; the few lights coming out of the apartment windows are also dim. The effect is not really gloomy or grim, this Eastern European darkness. The lack of bright artificial lights in cities at night takes some getting used to, but then it becomes a part of the atmosphere, sometimes even warm and comforting. The dark is stark in a blunt sense, creating a contemplative tone. It seems easier to think without a barrage of visual information, whether that information is the light of Western advertising signs or just bright streets that require no work to see.

We head around a corner and then into a passageway that is not just dim, it is pitch black. It is so dark that it is hard to see the door that Krísti pushes open for us. He laughs, pointing out the broken glass in the door, and makes his way up a flight of equally black steps.

At the top of the steps he pushes open another door, revealing a jammed restaurant, row after row of tables heaped with food and wine and beer. At the back of the long room an electric band featuring a violin is playing "I Did It My Way."

The Frank Sinatra tune only adds to the mystery of the place. Why is it unmarked? How bizarre that the generous dinner for the three of us costs only five deutsche marks, about a dollar each. "Why is there no sign on this restaurant?" I ask Krísti.

The question is a difficult one for him. "Why should there be a sign?" is his response, because he knows that anyone who wants to eat at the place—except for the very few strangers passing through—knows where it is located.

The street degenerates quickly as we drive out of downtown Timişoara toward his cousins' house. Eventually the pavement ends, and we bounce along dodging potholes full of water and piles of rocks, finally pulling up in front of a concrete block building. We stumble through the dark, climb the stairs, and bang on the apartment door. It must be past eleven. Nonetheless the hospitality is unquestioning. Just a year earlier such an invitation to a foreigner—without reporting it to the police—was illegal. Even an unreported passing contact with a foreigner on a Romanian street was against the law under Ceauşescu; penalties were fines and jail sentences.

The cousins insist on giving up their bed, which is really the couch in the tiny living room. Instead they want to sleep on the dinette bench in the tinier kitchen. The living room is dominated by a big black-and-white TV. In the kitchen there's no sign of a refrigerator; the only evidence of a cooking device is a hot plate, actually just an electric coil wandering through a concrete block. The rug is scraps of indoor-outdoor carpet. Dried, wilted flowers sit on a night table. The furniture is minimal: a kitchen table, a cupboard, not much else. It is poorly constructed out of plywood and covered with layers of chipping paint. What is immediately striking is that there is nothing in the apartment that suggests quality, permanence, or sentimental value. On the wall is a picture of a couple of cats that looks as if it's been torn out of a magazine.

We're ill equipped to reciprocate for hospitality, but Markos offers the host a couple of packs of Kents and offers his wife some shampoo and shower gel in individual bottles from some Intercontinental or Sheraton. The response to the shampoo and soap is not just polite. She is clearly thrilled to receive these luxury products, normally unavailable to her. Immediately she rushes into the bathroom to inspect them further and test them out.

The next morning we're up early, awakened by Romanian gypsy music screaming from the radio. The wife needs to get to her job at a butcher shop ("a meat laboratory," Krísti calls it in English).

So Krísti and I sit in the cramped kitchen, getting to know each other, getting insight into each other's cultures and societies. Various leaves are jammed in a pot and put to heat on the coil. A loaf of bread appears to go with the tea. Homemade jam shows up for the bread.

Krísti pulls out a map, shows me Soviet Moldavia, and forecasts another Eastern European crisis. Krísti expects that as the Soviet Union's central government weakens, Soviet Moldavia will gain its independence. Then, he says, because of the historical connections, it will unite with Romania. But that unification, he's convinced, will create severe social problems, because in Soviet Moldavia, "their industry and schools are backward, their living conditions no good, and they write with Cyrillic characters." It's hard to believe that he's criticizing others' housing and industry from the squalor of Timişoara.

We work through one of the opposition newspapers together. The banner headline — "High prices, not enough goods" — hangs over a picture of the door of a shop. Posted on the door is a sign: *Inchis Lipsa de Marfa* — Closed, Not Enough Goods. Another story details the misery of abandoned and sick children in an orphanage. The paper blames the Ceauşescu policies that forbade contraception. The pitiful state of sick children is one of the saddest legacies of the Romanian Communists. Ill and handicapped children without parents, or with parents unable to care for them, who were classified *nerecuperabli* — incurable — were dispatched to die in institutions with inadequate staffs and facilities.

It's my turn to show something. I drag a Canadian news-magazine out of my bag. Krísti feels the slick paper between his thumb and forefinger and just rubs it over and over again. It is a satisfying tactile opportunity for him.

"Quality." It's an unusual experience for him.

Page by page he works his way through the magazine.

"Beautiful," he murmurs at a Toyota advertisement.

He studies another ad promoting an arthritis remedy and is pleased with himself after figuring out what's being sold.

"We have medicine," he's a bit bewildered, "but no ads for it."

But it is on the cover where he really meets something new. He pores over the bar code, studying it, trying to figure out its significance.

★   ★   ★

The line of cars waiting to get out of Romania at the Yugoslav border must be a mile long. They are mostly Ladas, roof racks loaded with jerrycans of gas for the long journey, and many pull trailers. But the plates are all Soviet and Romanian and so we pass them by, this army of travelers, barely moving. Border formalities for Soviets and Romanians are tedious and expensive, often impossible. Yes, their own countries allow them to leave now, but their neighbors are not happy about these economic refugees. To get into Yugoslavia, they must produce two hundred dollars' worth of hard Western currency. It is part of an effort by Yugoslavians to slow the flood of Soviets and Romanians coming not just to look around and sell some things for the now convertible Yugoslav dinars but to try and find some work and maybe even stay in the more hospitable surroundings they find once they cross the border. Many make the trip on foot. They are in line at the checkpoint, patient, carrying over-stuffed plastic satchels, looking pleased and anxious and hopeful.

★   ★   ★

Even the guards want to get out.

"What do you have to declare?" asks the young customs man in fast, perfect English as we eased into the customs shed ahead of the waiting line-up of refugees. Our American passports and

German license plates rationalized our first-in-line status. The Soviets and Romanians did not balk at our line-busting. They know that compared with Germans and Americans, they are second-class citizens at this border. We enjoy privileges they don't, and after a lifetime of double standards, they accept the inequality mutely.

"Nothing." It is true, we bought nothing in Romania.

"Did you steal anything in Romania?" It seems an odd question.

"No."

"If you did, tell me, because I will find it. Are you spies?" The questions come rapid-fire.

"No."

"Do you know anyone who would like to adopt me?"

That catches us off guard. We figure it's a joke and laugh.

"I'm serious" is the quick response to our chuckles.

We try to keep the feeling light, "Which state would you like to go to?"

"Any one" is the no-nonsense reply.

"Any one but New Jersey," I advise, still trying to keep things from getting too heavy.

Seeing that we're not going to be his ticket out of Romania, the customs man explains with abrupt finality, "Anywhere but here."

★   ★   ★

Just past the Yugoslav checkpoint, just past the Marlboro poster, a worn-out-looking woman waits by the side of the road. There's a twinkle in her eyes, though, and some style to her dress. She's topped off with a fur cap, and her feet are puffing out of shiny black pumps. Her appearance sets her apart from most of the border crossers with their drab clothing.

"First time in Yugoslavia?"

"First time with a passport," and she makes a sly grin. "I went in 1988 to see my sister."

She made her way across the border from Romania illegally then, but the Yugoslavian border guards picked her up and sent her back home. So she spent a year and a half in a Ceauşescu prison for her unauthorized trip.

"Terrible. I want to go to Austria. But I can't get a visa. I want to work in Yugoslavia or Austria."

"What kind of work?"

"Any work." The answer is firm as she stands by the side of the road, with a pile of baggage, trying to get a ride a few kilometers into the first Yugoslavian border city to start a new life — still spirited, still smiling.

Chapter Eight

THE FUTURE IS NOW
IN YUGOSLAVIA

"Our national hobby has become a battle for freedom. All our longing for freedom has been used up in fighting for freedom."
—Yugoslav writer and poet Matija Beckovic, 1990

"DO YOU SPEAK English?"

It's a common greeting all over the world. Sometimes it's offered as a salutation: "You speak English!" The happy acknowledgment of a fellow traveler who overhears some familiar sounds. Other times, it's an imploring question, hoping for some common denominator that will help solve a problem.

That's what the gangling guy in the street of Mali Losinj was making clear. He wanted help. He thrust his hand out in greeting.

"My name's Pete. I'm from New York." Losinj is a Yugoslavian island in the Adriatic. The sky is deep blue, so is the water. In July and August the beaches are flooded with German tourists, but the rest of the year the pace is slow. In the Venetian harbor, a few cafés spill out onto the sidewalk. One good show is the ice-cream man, who throws the scoops up in the air and lands them solidly on the cone. Then he feigns spilling the whole thing as he hands it over to the customer, grabbing it at the last second. Another show to watch is the docking of the rusty ferries that make their way up and down the coast.

Pete had just hopped off the bus and couldn't communicate with the woman in the tourist bureau. He was trying to get himself a room for the night and figure out how to find a ferry over to another little island where his grandparents were born and raised.

"I'm looking for my roots," he explained as the information came cascading from him. His grandmother is in her nineties. She doesn't remember much, but he heard stories about the island when he was a kid. He's touring Europe, visiting a sister in Spain and a cousin in Ireland. He wants to check with the courthouse on his grandparents' island, learn about them, see where they came from.

All this came out of him as we walked the block along the waterfront to the tourist office. He talked with the speed and pleasure of someone who's been traveling alone too long without a language to use with the other passengers on the bus. And he spoke with the gregarious openness of an American kid.

Just before we came to the tourist bureau, a couple came out of the government office next door: bride and groom. Relatives threw rice and snapped pictures.

"I have to stop and take a picture." Pete put down his duffel bag and rummaged around in it. By the time he came up with the camera, the newlyweds had passed him by. He ran back to them and, using hand gestures, made them stop and pose. Before they had any idea what was going on, he had his pictures, and we made our way into the tourist office to secure his room and boat information.

Pete was enjoying himself; he was smiling and happy.

"This doesn't seem like a Communist country!"

In fact, this part of Yugoslavia was just voting the Communists out.

★   ★   ★

It is easy to enjoy the splendors of the Adriatic coast completely unaware of the murderous turmoil of Yugoslavian politics and the difficult economy. The water and sky are that calming deep blue, the beaches soft and inviting. The coastline and the general mentality are far from the gritty gray of so much of Eastern Europe.

The city of Rijeka is closer to that gray grit. "If you like punishment," warns David Stanley in *Eastern Europe on a*

Shoestring, "Rijeka will give it to you." We were robbed in that
port city on our way to the island paradise. It is a tough-looking
city, and we made sure the car was parked in a safe place, a
special blocked-off street used by the hotel. Not safe enough.

The first indication of the break-in came the next morning.
The passenger side window was open; then we saw that the
wind-wing was broken, and we called the cops.

Certainly American big city police, with their fast squad cars
and computers hooked up to FBI headquarters, rarely manage
to capture the bums who break into cars. But watching the work
of two Rijeka detectives was a reminder of how much catching
up the Eastern bloc is faced with.

They walked across town from their station house to the hotel
to meet with us. Actually they ambled. Then we all went out to
the car and made up a list of what was missing: clothing, camera,
tape recorder, my son Michael's Christmas presents. One of the
cops took out his detective's kit and with a little brush and some
silver powder started searching for fingerprints. The silver
powder stains are still all over the camper. After much sign
language about what was lost and how distressing it is to be
robbed, we all trudged back over to the police station, where, on
a manual typewriter with a stack of carbon paper for the copies,
the police report was laboriously pecked out in Croatian. The
detailed report included not just what happened, what was lost,
and my name and address, but also my father's name.

The omnipresent use of the father's name on all documents is
another subtle reminder of the great difference between Eastern
European and American culture. In America, it is our birthright
to start over. It is an important aspect of our society that, at least
officially and in principle, the identity of a person's father is
unimportant to any issue at hand. We stand or fall based on who
we are and our own personal performance. That is not so in the
old country, where they are forever tied—for better or for
worse—with their lineage.

The doorman at the hotel was concerned about the shattered
wind-wing. He made a template of the opening from cardboard
and then reappeared from the hotel with a replacement window

he cut from some scrap Plexiglas. He would not let me do any of the work, insisting on taping the plastic window in place himself, all the while apologizing for the robbery, clearly distressed that it would leave us with a bad feeling about Rijeka. It did, despite his nice work and good intentions.

"Just like New York," Michael assessed the place with disgust.

That morning in Rijeka I found a typical example of the kind of make-work employment that guaranteed so many Eastern Europeans a paycheck. I saw a little red toy Lada in a store window and went in to buy it. The store was all but empty of customers, and there were three clerks. I pointed to the toy car I wanted. The first clerk I encountered wrote up my purchase on a receipt (with several copies, of course). She then handed the Lada to the wrapping clerk and sent me across the floor to the cashier. I gave my pile of receipts to the cashier and paid for the car. At least two of the receipts came back to me, and I was directed back across the store to the wrapping clerk. There I surrendered one of the tickets for the Lada, neatly wrapped in coarse paper, folded tightly to save use of any tape or string.

This was nothing unique for Rijeka. All across the Communist East, such featherbedding kept the natives somewhat pacified with something to do. Now that competitive merchandising is taking over, buying toys and everything else is getting much faster. But the wrapping clerk and the cashier are looking for work.

The robbery quickly lost importance. We drove away from Rijeka somewhat aimlessly, cruising along the coast. At first the road was lined with resorts, then they gave way to open countryside. It was a twisting two-lane road. Rijeka became fainter and fainter, fading into the horizon as we followed a tiny side road down to the water, the road marked with a ferry sign. At the ferry landing was a lone café. We asked the fellow making bitter espresso what was on the other side. All we could see was the profile of an island in the distance, with nothing particular to distinguish it.

"Paradise," he announced without hesitation. "Go there! It is beautiful. You will love it. You will have a great time!"

The boat goes across Kvarner Bay from Brestova to Porozina in just about an hour. It's another rusting little tub, looking precarious as the trucks and buses roll onto it, making it list for the crossing. No one seems concerned about balancing the load. The mood is relaxed. There's beer down below in a dark café, or salt air and benches up on the top deck.

Cres looms on the horizon with the promise of a dream vacation, a promise the island can keep. The luxury hotels are stuffed only in July and August. The rest of the year, the weather is still delightful, and the beaches are not jammed body to body with baking Germans. Life is okay for the locals, too. They make a decent dinar on the tourists, or by fishing, or from working in Germany and Austria and bringing the money home to spend.

"I have the best life," the "sport man" (as he called himself) at one of the island resort hotels told Sheila with a happy smile. "I am free from worry." It is a pretty cushy job for a young single fellow. He's in charge of the sports equipment at the hotel and spends his days renting rowboats, lazing on the beach, flirting with women guests and hanging out at the hotel's beachfront café. That the state, not he, owns the concession doesn't bother him at all. "It is better that I don't own these things," he says. "If the boat breaks, they fix it. If the car breaks, they fix it." And what about Yugoslavia's crisis-filled political situation? "It doesn't matter," he smiled again, insisting he was totally unconcerned about what was happening, convinced it would not affect him. He just repeated that he enjoys the best possible life because he doesn't own anything and doesn't have a wife.

"Just me and my dog," and he sauntered over to the café for another beer.

The village of Cres is nestled on the shore of a sun-washed bay. At dawn the fishermen go out, the engines of their open boats chugging with a calm, throaty pulse that reverberates securely through the harbor. As the day gets warmer, the old men—the ones who don't go out fishing any longer—lounge on a long bench in front of the post office, looking out to sea. Wearing matching, jaunty berets, they smoke and watch, sometimes talking, but often just silent. Children skip through the streets. Once in a while the bus to Rijeka shows up and casually takes on passengers.

Later in the day the few bars — each with a reminder picture of Tito — fill up with men, smoke, and card games.

The mustard-colored Cres Hotel sits on the quay. The view is perfect, across the harbor and over the fishing boats to the Venetian-style houses and shops on the other side, the mountains and the sea farther away in the distance. This is not a tourist hotel; transient Yugoslavs use it, and travelers on a tight budget. The rooms are on the second floor, furnished with sagging beds and a table and chairs; below is a restaurant. The restaurant is divided into two dining rooms. One is jammed with Cres locals, eating, drinking, watching the news on the loud TV. The other room is empty; it's for the tourists. The food is the same, the price at least double. But the mood is so serene, the sights so spectacular, the weather so perfect, that it is difficult to complain about the double standard.

Especially after the bleakness of so much of the rest of Eastern Europe, the colors of the Yugoslavian coast are breathtaking. The sky always seems that deep blue, matching the water, that luscious Mediterranean blue that makes both sky and sea look so rich and comforting. Dropping right down to the water are the pristine Venetian villages with their sun-bleached houses clustered around the fishing boat docks.

Valun is one of these idyllic villages, almost lost across Valun Bay from Cres. "Good-bye Valun, my dearest pride," mourns a favorite local folk song, "You fill all with yearning. Good-bye village and young maidens with your rounded breasts. If breasts were for sale, the boys would sell all they have to buy the girls' breasts."

Life cannot be as hard in these surroundings as it is in the inland cities, no matter what the political problems.

★ ★ ★

By the end of 1990 Yugoslavia was on the brink of civil war, or at least falling apart into several separate nations, nations that might not even continue to maintain any sort of federation with one another. At the same time, prices had escalated to the levels of Western Europe, often rising even higher. Traffic jams were clogging the border crossings into Italy and Austria, as frustrated Yugoslavians realized that food and clothing were usually less expensive at discount stores in those countries than at home and were often of higher quality.

On the shopping streets of Belgrade the stores fought against competition from cheaper street vendors. The black market had disappeared, because the dinar was pegged to the deutsche mark at a high rate, making it the first convertible Eastern European currency. Twenty-five dollars' worth of dinar bought a pair of Hungarian-made Levis. Just a Coke, a salad, bread, and cheese for lunch cost five dollars in a decent restaurant. *Sexy* magazine was on sale, sealed in a blue plastic wrapper, with a free condom thrown in as a premium.

Yugoslavia's independent attitude has always kept its story different from the rest of the Eastern bloc. Yugoslavia suffered massive losses after Hitler invaded. Tito and his Communist partisans fought throughout World War II against the Axis and the puppet fascist government set up in Croatia. That fighting was an extension of the conflicts among the nationalities that make up Yugoslavia, fighting that's been going on as long as stories about the Balkans have been told.

Because of his powerful army and personality, Tito was able to force the Yugoslavs to get along while he was alive and running the country. He rejected Soviet influence back in 1948 and carved out an independent foreign policy and Communist Party–controlled economy. The government enjoyed economic assistance from the West, influenced world politics by attempting to avoid aligning with either West or East, and offered its citizens substantial personal freedom compared with the other Eastern European societies.

Probably the most important freedom, for the people and for Yugoslavia, was the right to travel out of the country. Travel enabled Yugoslavians to go to West Germany and the rest of Western Europe and earn hard currency. Much of the money made its way back to Yugoslavia, improving the standard of living. When workers came home, along with the money, they brought Western ideas. Yugoslavians did not suffer the isolation that for such a long time plagued the other Eastern Europeans left behind the Iron Curtain.

Tito's picture still glares out from the walls of shops and restaurants all over the country. Often it's a harsh black-and-white line drawing, showing Tito with an irritated expression on his face, looking annoyed that the Yugoslavian nation he forged has been degenerating since he died in 1980.

The Serbs hate the Croats, especially because of the Croats' alliance with the Nazis. Serbs claim that their relatives living in enclaves of Croatia are mistreated. Croatians insist that the Serbs misuse their power in the central government and take resources from other republics to improve Serbia. Croatia, with its tourist-packed Adriatic coast, is richer than Serbia and voted early in 1990 to get rid of its Communist government. The Serbs want more land and grab at provinces within Serbia that are supposed to be autonomous, particularly Kosovo. The ethnic Albanians there look forward to the demise of the Albanian Communist government in Tirana and the development of a Greater Albania that would include Kosovo, giving the ethnic Albanians in Kosovo leverage against the infiltrating Serbs. The Slovenians are busy getting even richer than the Croatians by interacting with Austria and the rest of Western Europe and don't think they need to send their tax dollars away to the rest of Yugoslavia. Many Slovenians feel much more affinity for Austrians and their way of life than with the other Yugoslav republics. By the spring of 1990, they too had voted out their Communist provincial government and made it clear that they'd prefer to make their way as an independent country.

Those are just the major players. Other nationalities and family feuds are at work in Yugoslavia and are not just confined within the country's current borders. Plenty of Macedonians wouldn't like just a separate country from their fellow Yugoslavians, they'd like to add territory now in Greece and Bulgaria that they consider part of historical Macedonia.

The lack of trust and the bad relations inside Yugoslavia are matched by paranoia about what's across the national borders.

In his column in the Serbian newspaper *Politika,* Marko Lopusina worries that "the mass defecting of Albanians from the Tirana regime is not a spontaneous, panic-stricken reaction of unhappy people, but a well-planned move made by the leadership in Tirana. Stories of how some of them walked thirty kilometers to the border and freely passed the Albanian border guards," writes Lopusina, "sound incredible, bearing in mind the fact that the same border guards shoot Albanian citizens at the Albanian-Greek border."

He suggests there might be a conspiracy to create the Greater Albania at the expense of Yugoslavia: "Not a single Serb, Montenegrin, or Macedonian has escaped illegally" is Lopusina's argument, "only ethnic Albanians. Why do Albanian refugees escape only to Yugoslavia?"

It is a mess, a mess so volatile that late in 1990 the CIA issued an unusual report forecasting the demise of Yugoslavia during the early nineties after a messy fight. The CIA gave Yugoslavia no more than a year and a half before the union collapsed and predicted that the country would fall apart, not by agreement or at the ballot box, but in a bloody civil war. There is fear throughout the rest of newly liberated Eastern Europe that if those dire predictions come true, the developing democracies throughout the region will also be in jeopardy. Keeping a lid on nationalistic and ethnic rivalries is as important a concern for Yugoslavia and the rest of the old Eastern bloc as are the pollution crisis and the eviscerated economies. And in Yugoslavia, the tale takes one more bizarre twist, because Serbia, still run by the powerful Communist government (renamed for public relations reasons the Socialists), is at odds with its post-Communist Croatian and Slovenian neighbors. Additional complications are created because the Serbian Communists control the army. This makes the conflict not just historical, ethnic, and territorial, but also political. No wonder the CIA is pessimistic.

★ ★ ★

If you are rich or equipped with a fat expense account, you can spend a comfortable night in Belgrade at the Intercontinental or the Hyatt. Both are brand-new and no different from their counterparts in the West. But if you're looking for a bargain, about the best you can do is the offensive Trim Hotel, labeled the cheapest accommodation in the capital city. In late 1990, that translated to fifty-five U.S. dollars for a crummy little room with cracked windows, sockets empty of light bulbs, and a bold cockroach population.

The Arab refugee living a few rooms down came over as we were moving in our bags.

"Park your car right next to the window, here," he advised, pointing to the little patio. "That way you can hear when it is being molested."

The desk clerk is a dumpy, stern, Stalinist woman, no smiles and all business in her official blue desk clerk uniform. She studies my passport laboriously, searching for the stamp that shows through which border crossing we entered Yugoslavia. She is irritated that she cannot read the stamp and that we cannot remember the name of the crossing. Finally, her irritation peaks as she realizes there really is nothing she can do about the fact that she cannot read the name, so with disgust she takes our money and registers us.

Life is hard these days for the old Communist workers who bought into the rigid Stalinist system. So much of what they learned and accepted and maybe even believed in—like slow bureaucratic controls on things as mundane as checking into a hotel—is passing into history.

★   ★   ★

Though it is not quite yet winter 1990, already the wind is sharp and whips the frosty air. But the uncomfortable weather doesn't discourage the politicians lining Kneza Mihaila, the main drag in Belgrade. The Communists are still in control of the government in Serbia, but the opposition finally is free to work the crowds.

"For forty-five years all we have had is Marx and Lenin," complains Zoran Dragovic. He's a twenty-five-year-old waiter soliciting signatures on a petition already jammed with names. "We want a new curriculum in the school that teaches about religion. We have many people who need to learn about God."

Which god? Which religion?

"That plays no role." Dragovic's reply is instant. "Catholic, Orthodox, what's written in the Koran — all. Today that is not in school."

He does pick a favorite religion for himself. He's selling buttons of Serbia's patron saint, Saint Sava. "The Communists have had a monopoly and taught that Marxism is the only way. Here in Serbia there is no Christian party. But there is Saint Sava, the first teacher."

As with so much in Eastern Europe, his cause just went public. He's been at his card table seeking signatures for only three hours. Proudly he shows off the filled pages, just three hours and already 952 names are on his list.

"The Communists go in the church in the past, see who is in the church, and arrest them. But now is a new time. Thank God."

Just a few feet away is the next table. There the ultranationalist Chetnik organization is at work. The group is still illegal as a political party because Tito and the Communists blamed them — and the Croatian fascist organization Ustashi — for much of the internal killing that occurred in Yugoslavia during World War II. Slobodan Savic is working the Chetnick table, selling car stickers to replace the YU national stickers that Yugoslavian cars wear. His read SER and, just to make sure the message is not lost, say "State of Serbia" on the bottom. He's selling all sorts of Serbian nationalist paraphernalia: eagle pins with crowns, an opposition newspaper with the headline "Not Yugoslavia, Serbia!" and posters of the Chetnick leader Vojslav Sheshelj.

Sheshelj is in jail for violating the law against engaging in Chetnick-associated political activities. But on the street, Savic is undeterred. "I think most Serbian people want to legalize this party. I want to legalize this party because I am a Serbian. Sheshelj wants to make Serbia on top!"

Savic insists he just wants to help out his fellow Serbians, "Serbians in Croatia. They haven't got their rights there."

He's optimistic a solution can be found but convinced there is only one alternative to satisfying the desires of the Serbians living in Croatia. "I think it will be compromise with Croatia, or there will be war. If we win the war, everyone in Yugoslavia will be equal. If we lose the war, it will be the end of Yugoslavia." He thinks for a minute more and adds, "I would like that there will not be a war."

Knin is one of those Serbian enclaves surrounded by Croatians. It's tucked in the mountains between Split on the coast and the Croatian capital Zagreb. Toward the end of 1990, Markos had some experience with the trigger-ready Serbs in Knin. He made his way through the mountains, the highway lined with the Croatian, not the Yugoslavian, flag. That flag is highlighted by its red-and-white checkerboard shield. Even the symbol adds to the conflict between the Serbs and Croats. Serbians say the shield resembles too closely the mark used by the Ustashi fascists during World War II, and makes them fear today's Croatians as their parents feared those a generation back.

Roadblocks on the outskirts of Knin slowed Markos's car, with the other traffic, allowing Serbian guards posted along the highway to get a good look at travelers before they entered Knin. Other guards closer to the town — these armed with shotguns — stopped cars and checked the drivers, demanding to see identification and to know the purpose of the trip. The border patrol was not keeping Croatians out of the Serbian town, just establishing territory and adding to the tension throughout Yugoslavia that was being generated by the political leaders and their talk of conflict and separation.

Once inside Knin, Markos, going to an interview with a Serbian leader, made his way through the old Balkan downtown, where most of the menfolk went about their daily business with a mean-looking automatic pistol stuffed down their pants. During the interview, the talk turned to the Croatian president, Franjo Tudjman, and the Knin Serbian leader pulled his pistol out and leveled it at Markos's head to make sure his point was clear. "I'm saving this," he said as he aimed the gun at Markos, "for Tudjman."

The conflict is difficult. If Croatia goes solo, what does happen to the Serbians stuck in places like Knin, Serbians who feel so threatened? That's why the powerful Serbians — and the Yugoslavian army is dominated by Serbs — want to enlarge Serbia to include those pockets of their population, like Knin, that are outside the current political lines of the Serbian republic.

* * *

"Where are you going?"

The money changer in Nis is cheery.

"Sofia," we answer.

"Sofia and then on to Greece?"

"No, Sofia."

"And on to Turkey?" he asks.

"No, just Sofia."

He can't quite believe the destination, until I tell him we're journalists, and then he's ready to talk, not about Bulgaria, but Yugoslavia.

"What will happen?" I ask him.

"*Que serà, serà*," he smiles. His English is nearly perfect. He takes time out from stacking bills. His job is not so complex since the Yugoslav government pegged the dinar to the deutsche mark. The nonstop inflation of the past several years is calming, ever-increasing stacks of dinar are no longer needed daily to swap for Western money.

"Let me tell you a story." He's clearly pleased to have an American audience, and he's geared up to explain Yugoslavia's problems from his Serbian perspective.

"Say a man has a brother and the man has some things and the brother nothing. So the man gives his brother a suit of clothes. And then after a while the brother gets some money and says, 'This suit is shit,' and throws it away and goes and buys a new one from someone else."

He stops. I wait, but he's silent, so I ask, "And the brother is Croatia?"

"Maybe."

But he's not just riled about Croatia.

"Without Serbia the others would not be states. Our kings were always crowned in Kosovo. We're not giving that up. Slovenians have a state. It is Austria."

★   ★   ★

By the end of 1990, there was little going on inside Yugoslavia to suggest that the conflicts in the patched-together state would be settled peacefully and less to suggest that Yugoslavia would continue to exist as a political unit. Instead, the world watched and worried about another balkanization of the Balkans.

Chapter Nine

BULGARIA'S
SECOND REVOLUTION

"Hope for the best. Expect the worst."

— Young Bulgarian career woman musing about her future,
Winter 1990

"We dream of November 1991, when all this will be part of the past."

— Journalist Milena Boyadjieva, writing in the *Sofia News*,
November 1990

BULGARIA WAS RUNNING out of cigarettes by the end of 1990. This was an absurd crisis in the Balkan country. Just like people all over the Eastern bloc, Bulgarians smoke incessantly. Unlike the rest of the Eastern bloc, Bulgaria grows and exports tobacco. And at the end of 1990, unlike the rest of the Eastern bloc, Bulgaria was still ruled by a Communist government.

The offer of a cigarette started just about every conversation.

"Do you smoke?" asked the international relations director of the Bulgarian Peace Party. We were in his sparsely furnished office. Actually sparse is too generous a word. There was nothing, not even heat, in the dark wood-paneled room except a scattering of chairs, a table and a desk. There was nothing on the desk, no pictures on the walls, no books on the shelves. The adjoining office boasted one telephone and an old typewriter.

"No, I'm from California," was again my response. He offered his own explanation for lighting up.

"I'm smoking now because it is very cold. We have no heat. I have no electric blanket."

He was bundled up in a turtleneck sweater, a jacket, and wool pants, spending his time philosophizing vaguely about utopian governments.

"We have no time to be on the tail of life. We have to jump with mentality to change old-fashioned thinking. We have no choice. We have no choice. Of course everything must be democratic. But what is democracy? There is only one kind of democracy. If we follow this path of democracy, we will come to the highway of normal life. I don't want to say 'new life' because that was a slogan of the Communists, but normal life."

The next day the offer of a cigarette came from one of the leaders of the student strike.

"Do you smoke?"

"No, thanks."

"We are just like prisoners," he said, lighting up, "smoking, smoking, smoking."

Over the next few days, cigarettes explained Bulgaria as much as anything could.

There were no crowds at the Bulgarian border as we drove in from Yugoslavia. The car was not searched. Remnants of the gates and barricades that used to restrict travel in and out of the country were lying by the side of the road. The foundations for the barriers had been jackhammered away; the piles of broken concrete were just left alongside the road.

Only days before, visa requirements for Americans traveling to Bulgaria had been lifted. The guards were still getting used to the new rules. The border station looked like a dilapidated row of turnpike tollbooths. In each lane, immediately after the passport check was another hut housing the bank. The clerk there wanted us to change thirty dollars into Bulgarian leva for every day we were staying in the country.

"It's obligatory."

This, too, was a legacy from the old days that was ending faster than the bureaucracy could keep track. We balked at her demand, saying we didn't need to change so much money.

"What did the policeman say?" she asked.

"Nothing," we told her. It was true.

"Okay." She waved us into Bulgaria.

The next blockade was a wooden hut adorned with a hand-painted sign advising that the road to Sofia required an eleven-dollar (dollar, not lev)[1] payment. We eased the car forward, and the man standing at the hut waved us on, free.

* * *

When revolution cascaded across Eastern Europe in 1989, the thirty-five-year-long Todor Zhivkov dictatorship fell with the rest. The people celebrated their new freedom and called an election. Zhivkov's old Communist Party cronies quickly renamed themselves the Socialists. They convinced a majority of the voters that a future with an unknown government would be worse than leaving the old bureaucrats in charge. The voters, freed from Zhivkov as a personal symbol of oppression and enjoying intellectual freedom unknown since World War II, decided to give the Communists another try. Bulgaria became the only Eastern bloc country to overthrow their Communist dictators in 1989 and then elect them to replace themselves in 1990.

By the end of 1990, most Bulgarians realized that they had made a terrible mistake. Basic food, like flour and sugar, was in short supply. Rolling power blackouts kept Sofia without electricity for hours on end; gasoline lines wrapped around corners and ran for blocks.

The Balkantourist office in Sofia is around the corner from the Sheraton Hotel at Knjaz Dondukov 37. From the street it looks closed, so few lights are turned on. Inside, it is quiet, that subdued quiet familiar to public places in Eastern European. This hushed atmosphere seems to be a cultural affirmation that loud displays in public are inappropriate combined with leftover concerns about being overheard.

A few bare fluorescent tubes burn, giving just enough light to do business. The counters need paint; the upholstered chairs

---

[1] *Lev* is the singular form of *leva*.

are threadbare. The linoleum, laid in sheets, is separating and buckling at the seams. There is one wire brochure rack. It's empty.

An American can't stay just anywhere in Sofia. The Sheraton is available for well over a hundred dollars a night, so is the somewhat dilapidated Novotel. But most second-class Bulgarian hotels are off-limits to American travelers, another remnant from the old regime, a detail that keeps hard Western currency flowing into Bulgaria. Americans must pay for their overnight stays with dollars or other convertible Western money.

There is an alternative to the expensive hotels. Through the government tourist office, arrangements can be made to rent a room in a private home.

"I'm warning you, because it is on the thirteenth floor, you have to be careful," the clerk looked concerned as she took less than ten dollars for the room and handed over the keys, explaining the shortages plaguing Bulgaria.

"Careful, the electric goes out. It is very difficult. You can't cook. You can't work."

The struggling Communist government was dealing with energy shortages by sweeping power blackouts through Sofia. Every couple of hours, the electricity would cut out in various neighborhoods for a couple of hours. The schedule was erratic; nobody knew for sure when and for how long the power would be out. The Iraqi invasion of Kuwait was the second of a one-two energy punch that hit Bulgaria late in 1990. Iraq owed a huge debt to Bulgaria and was paying it off in oil. After the invasion, the blockade of Iraq kept Bulgaria from getting that oil, and it had no money to buy other oil on the expensive open market. Bulgaria had already reneged on its foreign debt. The first punch came from the Soviet Union, which stopped supplying Bulgaria with cheap oil and insisted on payment in hard currency, currency Bulgaria lacked.

So taxis waited in the gas lines that snaked around corners and extended for several blocks. Taxi drivers worked a day driving, and then spent the next day waiting in a gas line.

The clerk at Balkantourist is sad to report the state of her country. "People are not very happy. We are not very happy here. We have a winter ahead. You don't know what is ahead of you."

She tries to offer help, advice to the uninitiated traveler.

"You can still buy bread freely, for the time being. Flour, butter, and eggs are rationed, and you need coupons. Coupon number eleven for flour. Number one for sugar. One kilogram for one person for one month. That is why it is very complicated to be a tourist here."

But the apartment is convenient and comfortable. The landlady is a plump older woman. She speaks just enough English. The extra bedroom she rents is small. But unlike the Balkantourist office, here all the sparse furnishings are in good repair, and the place is spotless. From the tiny balcony the Sofia skyline disappears into smog. And periodically, without warning, the lights go out.

The hallway is an abrupt contrast with the apartment. Years of deferred maintenance have turned it into the hallway of a slum. The paint is curling off the walls in big patches, just peeling away from years of disinterest and neglect. There are two elevators, but the power blackouts are not their only problems. Obviously one of the lifts has not operated for a long time. Pots of scraggly-looking, thirsty flowers sit in front of the elevator doors, not just on our landing, but on others, too. It is a vain attempt to add some cheer to the depressing entryways; it generates the opposite effect, just a reminder that the elevator is broken.

Down on street level, the lobby is no better. The plate glass is broken in the front doors, leaving jagged holes for the cold. It's dark, even during the day. It is in front of the apartment house that I first notice something missing from all the parked cars. After studying them for a minute I realize what it is. No parked car has windshield wipers. Drivers keep their wiper blades inside the car, only clipping them on when it rains or snows; otherwise, they're stolen.

In the dark streets, as they roll slowly past the crumbling downtown, the cars without wipers add another layer to the oddness.

* * *

It is evening—dark in what is still called Lenin Square. Lenin's statue is mostly ignored. It towers next to a construction site, and a temporary fence runs along two sides of the pedestal, reducing the majesty of the soaring sculpture. The splotches of paint thrown on Lenin mock his authoritarian presence, and the fresh flowers left by the Party faithful can't compensate. The flowers take on a pitiful appearance in contrast to the paint; the official Party ribbons around the bouquets become just a reminder that the flowers are ordered by the Party propaganda machine, while the paint is clearly thrown spontaneously by frustrated Bulgarians.

A crowd is forming in Lenin Square. Some hold signs against the government. "Socialists equal Communists!" is the message. In front of the party headquarters building, chanting starts: "Down with the Communist Party! Bulgarian Communist Party to Siberia for Peace! Bulgarian Communist Party is Mafia! The time is finished!"

I wander around as the crowd builds, finding people who speak English. "Most of the people in our country oppose the Socialist government, so whenever there is a meeting many people come," one women tells me. And what will happen? "They will talk and talk. They only talk.

"Where are you from?" she asks.

"California." It is a magic word in all languages.

"Ah, California," she looks wistful; "it is beautiful there, I guess."

"Yes." I can't lie, even if she is stuck in a freezing Bulgarian winter with no food, no gas, no electricity, no cigarettes, and little hope.

"This is not beautiful," she points to the Communist Party headquarters. It is a massive Stalinist-style building, barricaded from the crowds, still suffering from the scars of a fire set during a similar demonstration a few months before.

I find a student who speaks some English. "People are crazy because there is not enough food," he tells me as the chanting gets louder. University students are on strike, he says, "because after the elections they don't give nothing to the Bulgarian people. I think Bulgaria, after 10 November [the date Zhivkov was overthrown], nothing changed. The people don't want to live like before."

The students are lighting candles, holding them in plastic cups, starting to form a single picket line along the perimeter of huge Lenin Square. Another chant starts: "We don't want to study for rats!"

Then a few students try to calm the crowd and quiet the screaming chanters, especially a few rowdies who carry themselves with the tough self-confidence that suggests they easily could be provocateurs. It's always an important problem, trying to determine who are the real opposition, and who are the provocateurs assigned by the ruling power to cause trouble and discredit the opposition.

"This is a meeting of students. We must keep silence. Don't scream," pleads one intense fellow. The crowd chants back anyway. He's carrying a candle in a cup, wearing jeans and sneakers. His beard is scruffy; his eyes dance around the crowd, full of the moment. A white scarf is loosely knotted around his neck. "Liverpool" is woven into it.

"I'm here because I don't want to live like before," he tells me. This was my introduction to Marian Valav, one of the leaders of the student strike. He studies acting at the Academy of Theater while he performs professionally around Bulgaria. He is intense, speaking fast, and in just a few minutes tries to summarize what he is doing and why: "I want a normal life like in other countries . . . I do everything I can do, but I haven't power . . . What can we change with this meeting? Nothing, you see, nothing . . ."

Marian acknowledges and dismisses the freedoms that came to Bulgaria at the end of 1989 with the overthrow of Zhivkov. "I can talk about everything; that is no problem now. There is pseudo-democracy here. No one is listening."

Marian and his colleagues are convinced that it was their strike during the summer that brought down the Communist president of the country. The current president, Zhelyu Zhelev, is a member of the opposition. Zhelev is appreciated as a philosopher; he wrote a book denouncing Communism back when such an act was considered treason. But his opposition and the Communist/Socialist majority in the parliament cannot come to any compromise. The inaction is aggravating Bulgaria's troubles.

In fact, many watching Bulgaria say the Communists are dragging their feet, intentionally not working to solve problems. That theory suggests the Communists know that their days are numbered; consequently, they just want to hold on to power as long as they can. The other theory takes the first one step further and suggests the Communists are busy building their own personal futures. They're laundering money, financing escapes, positioning themselves for roles in the coming market economy.

About bringing down the Communist president, Marian tells me, "We understand it is not enough to bring down one Communist, because there are always more."

He talks nonstop. "This demonstration is to break down the Communist government and rise up another government with a good program to satisfy simple needs. They promised us bread, liberty, justice. It was the big lie of the Communist Party."

Marian is impassioned, and it's not just his acting experience. "I can't take it no more!" he says. The candles flicker; the sound of chanting is replaced by the footsteps of the pickets circling Lenin Square. The police finger their billy clubs; the scorch marks on the party headquarters building look ominous.

In the adjoining Sheraton Hotel, the demonstration can't be heard or seen; the windows face away from the square. Instead of long lines for basic food and drink, luxury imports fill the tables, but only available for those spending hard Western currency. At the piano bar, the bored player is cranking out Elvis: "I can't help falling in love with you . . ."

There's no electricity across Sofia, but the flow of current never stops for the foreign guests in the Sheraton. The cute waitress smiles, "You want tea? Black or peppermint? Coffee? Espresso or cappuccino? Juice? Orange or pineapple? Wine? How about a Bulgarian dry white?"

Just hearing that so many choices are available is disorienting after wandering the streets seeing the closed and empty shops and the long lines for the most basic staples.

She smiles, "You will pay me in hard currency."

The businessman's lunch at the Sheraton goes for twenty-five dollars. The average worker's wage in Bulgaria is two hundred leva a month. On the black market a Bulgarian can buy a dollar for fifteen to twenty leva, so that twenty-five-dollar lunch costs about two and a half months' work.

The demonstration is over. The city is dim. The streetcars clatter through the streets, side panels held together with the equivalent of Bondo, desperately needing paint. Jammed with passengers, the trams run without lights. Clearly, the lights aren't out because of the blackouts; it is the fault of deferred maintenance. Here and there a headlight shines or a taillight glows, but the overall effect of the trams passing through the dark streets, carefully crossing intersections where the traffic lights and street lights both are off, adds to the surreal atmosphere in Sofia.

★   ★   ★

The University of Sofia is the headquarters of the student strike that's spread all across Bulgaria. The strike committee office is thick with cigarette smoke, and debate. A fax machine sits on a desk, an attempt to link up with the rest of the world.

"We want help from international students, for moral support," the strikers say. "If there is help from another country, especially the U.S.A., there will be very good results."

But America is preoccupied with Saddam Hussein. As demonstrations in Sofia continue, Bulgaria barely makes the news in the States.

At the Academy of Theater, strikers are collecting money for soup kitchens. In the tiny strike committee office, Peter Todorov contemplates the rest of the world's lack of interest in Bulgaria's problems. He's convinced that most people don't know what's happening. "The Communist leader is walking around Europe and is saying the situation in Bulgaria is good—people have liberty and justice and plenty of bread. He tells

Western Europe that there is democracy, that now the Communist Party is different."

Todorov's partner in the strike committee office is Dimitar Dimitrov. He's heard another story about how his government is trying to warp public opinion. "My girlfriend lives in Greece. A truck full of bananas and other soft fruit was turned back at the Bulgarian border because the government said there is no need for it. The fruit was donated by a Bulgarian businessman in Greece." How does he know this story is true? "The business-man is my girlfriend's cousin."

It's the kind of information the students fax around the world. They send daily reports to Radio Free Europe. They keep in touch with the Czech students who led the revolution that overthrew the Communist government in Prague. And they keep hoping the rest of the world will care and help.

There is a harsh reality, but also a sweetness to the student activities. Consider the November 10 "Statement of the Strike Committee of Sofia University." It is an explanation of why the students decided to occupy their campus as a device to force the government to change. "Only an occupational strike would guarantee that our protest will continue even after an eventual government change. It will continue until our demands have started to be satisfied, or at least until we have received firm guarantees on the part of the new government ensuring their solving over a short period of time." Then, following the signa-tures on the single-spaced typewritten statement comes this European apology: "Excuse us for the long statement, but we had no time for a shorter one."

That same day, representatives from schools all across the country issued what they called an "Appeal to the Bulgarian People." It is a moving document that reads like poetry:

> People, our maltreated Bulgaria is dying!
> The economy has collapsed! The soil and air are poisoned!
> The moral values are devalued!
> The young labor and intellectual power of Bulgaria is irre-
> trievably flowing out in all directions of the world.

Old people and children will be dying of starvation and cold, of lack of medicaments. Bulgaria is turning into a "waste land," with no past, somber present, and hopeless future.

We have to save our country!

Our protest was born out of pain!

With our strike we want to stop the stagnation, to overcome the destruction, to preserve the hope!

We are alone! Nobody stands behind us, except our civic duty.

The statement then explains why the students want the government changed and concludes with this plaintive call:

The time has come for those who caused the national crisis to hear at last the people's cry, to get ashamed and leave the stage.

We are your children, and we believe in you!

We want the future — help us for the present!

Other communiques from the strike committee reverberate with artful descriptions of Bulgaria's plight and poignant pleas for change. On October 25 came this missive: "Ex-'sister' nations overcame with one blow the resistance of their *nomenklatura*, took away stolen goods and handed over to justice the perpetrators, took successfully actions on the decision adopted for market reforms and started confidently to United Europe — and we are standing at the 'queue' again. Future becomes more gloomy and sad, people avert their eyes from us, calling us 'a red reserve.' Fetched to that dark present Bulgaria remains with no future."

The cry on the leaflet continues, "Faced with an economic and social deadlock, moral degradation, international isolation, and futureless life, we must understand clearly — IF WE DON'T HELP OURSELVES, NOBODY ELSE WILL DO IT FOR US!!!"

★   ★   ★

We're in one of the fanciest restaurants in Sofia. The maitre d' keeps the door locked with a magazine shoved through the handles. Only when he sees foreigners with money does he open up. Marian Valav is smoking, talking about the shortage of cigarettes in tobacco-growing Bulgaria.

"My father has bucks." That means his father has access to hard Western currency. It is because his father was a champion boxer, a member of the privileged class. "My father has bucks, so sometimes I go into the Free Shops." The Free Shops are the stores that the Bulgarian government runs to earn hard Western currency from tourists or Bulgarians who have opportunities to get their hands on hard Western currency. The Free Shops are stocked with stereos, whiskey, Levis, and other goods not made in Bulgaria—and not generally imported into the country because the average Bulgarian does not earn enough money to pay for such expensive foreign merchandise. "My father has bucks, so sometimes I go to the Free Shops and buy cigarettes," says Marian.

"It is twisted here," and he explains the lopsided workings of the cigarette economy in Bulgaria. It is a glimpse of why the entire economic structure of the country has broken down.

"I am buying Bulgarian tobacco in the Free Shop. It is grown in Bulgaria and the cigarettes are manufactured in Bulgaria, manufactured into Marlboros, HB, and Philip Morris."

But these Marlboros are not sold in shops to the Bulgarian people; they are exported to West Germany. Then the Bulgarian government reimports these cigarettes, now in Marlboro packages and cartons, for sale in the Free Shops. The price is ninety-five cents a package—extremely high by Bulgarian standards, but worth it to smokers like Marian.

"Bulgarian Marlboro," he says, "is better than American Marlboro because the tobacco is better."

But that is just the official cigarette economy. Cigarettes play a key role in the Bulgarian black market. Marian knows the details. It is a complicated scam.

Smugglers buy Kent cigarettes in Sofia. They take them to Romania, where they are in demand, bribing the border guards with them to get the rest of the cigarettes over the border. Once in Romania they sell the Kents for Romanian currency, Romanian lei. Then, on the Romanian black market they sell the lei for Bulgarian leva. Lei are worth nothing in Bulgaria, but the Bulgarian lev is of value in Romania and is available to buy. Leva have value in Romania because Romanians want to travel to Bulgaria, a land with more opportunities for them than their own. Very few Bulgarians are interested in going to Romania, so there is no market for lei in Bulgaria.

The smugglers return to Sofia with their pockets full of leva and go into the Vietnamese ghetto. The Vietnamese — second-class citizens in Bulgarian society — suffer from a lack of medicine, and the smugglers take medicines with them into the ghetto. They combine the medicines and the leva, trading the Bulgarian money to shrewd Vietnamese traders at a rate of five or six leva for one U.S. dollar. The Vietnamese manage to collect dollars by taking advantage of their international connections. This transaction of leva into dollars is illegal for Bulgarians to make in an official bank unless they obtain special approval from the government. With their pockets full of U.S. dollars, the Bulgarians sell their dollars to other Bulgarians who want to buy things at the Free Shops, this time for fifteen to twenty leva to the dollar. These Bulgarians at the end of the chain who want to shop at the Free Shops are afraid to change the money for themselves in the Vietnamese neighborhood because of its dangerous reputation.

"It's a great game," smiles Marian. And it explains, at least in part, why amid the lines in the street for flour and sugar, walking past the empty shop windows, a few Bulgarian women are decked out in long fur coats and here and there Bulgarian men are hopping out of sporty BMWs.

It also explains the men hanging out on the outskirts of Sofia at the Free Shop, motel, and gas station. These Bulgarians are equipped with fat wads of deutsche marks in relatively small denominations, fifties and hundreds. They are offering to trade these bills for very large denominations, five hundreds and particularly thousand-mark notes. These men offer a 20 percent premium for the exchange. It is illegal for them to take the hard currency out of Bulgaria, and they want to go to Germany and buy Western cars. A few thousand-mark bills are much easier to hide than a fat roll of fifties.

But this trade is also a bit twisted. Once the hustlers come back to Bulgaria with their fancy German cars, there's no gas for them.

The Vietnamese ghettos in Eastern Europe are another legacy of the Communist period. Just as West Germany and some other Western European countries imported Turks and other guest workers to get their economies going, so did the Eastern European countries bring in Vietnamese. The Vietnamese came as part of trade deals between governments. They worked for the Vietnamese government performing tasks in Eastern Europe that resulted in goods from Europe being forwarded to Vietnam. When the governments behind the Iron Curtain started to fall, many Vietnamese scrambled to stay, realizing life under the new governments in Europe would undoubtedly be superior to what awaited them back home.

There's no love lost between guys like Marian and the Vietnamese. "We don't like them because they have money and they get our girls. I had a girl, and she went with a Vietnamese because he had money and he can take her dancing and drinking."

★   ★   ★

"Just call me Lady Pena," says the smiling woman taking care of business at the tourist office of the fading Europa Hotel in Sofia. It's part of the Novotel chain, but it is struggling under the failing Bulgarian economy. Nonetheless, it is a great place to hang out in during the power blackouts. Because it houses Western tourists, its grid, like the Sheraton's, is never turned off.

"Pena is short for my real name," she says. "It means 'stupid village woman' in Bulgarian, so it is very funny with Lady. Half of Sofia knows me as Lady Pena."

She is anything but stupid. "We don't have enough intelligent people in this country," she laments, "because they were all killed or they were forced out. Now our young people are leaving because there are no jobs here."

"Nice breakfast," I tell Lady Pena after coming out of the Europa dining room. And it's not too bad. For about a dollar, delicious slabs of Bulgarian feta cheese, piles of substantial bread, jam—just one flavor, plum—but plenty of it—yogurt, salads seemingly left over from dinner. Nothing fancy, but perfectly adequate.

"You think this is nice?" She is disgusted. "You should have seen it years ago, almost like Switzerland."

This is not a shy woman.

"If you ask my opinion, the king should come back, even though my great-grandparents, my grandparents, and my parents were Communists. He should come back and bring the country together."

★ ★ ★

There are long lines at the Aeroflot offices, passengers trying to get out of the country on tickets that they buy with soft Bulgarian currency. Lufthansa flies out of Sofia, too. But there are no lines at the Lufthansa office, where hard currency is required.

The other lines are for the bread store, long lines into the street. Some lines don't even lead into stores. The rationed foodstuffs, the flour and sugar and eggs, are distributed from the sidewalk. Long lines in the cold, old people bundled up against the wind are holding their few leva and their ration coupons. It is a grim sight.

Other people walk with purpose toward particular stores and then are surprised when they get to the door to find it locked, the shelves empty and a Closed sign on the door.

There are lines for books being sold from cartons on the street. The fastest-moving, longest line is for English-Bulgarian dictionaries. Bulgarians, like the rest of the Eastern bloc, know that English and German are the languages that they need to better their lives. The Russian that was obligatory for so many years in school is no longer important. The Bulgarians do not consider the time they spent studying Russian as much of a waste; Bulgarian and Russian are so close linguistically that learning Russian is not very difficult. But other Eastern Europeans regard the long years of studying Russian as a waste of time. "We learned it to pass tests, and then forgot it," I was told over and over behind the Iron Curtain. This language of the oppressor was rejected as a political statement. English was sought after as a language of hope, an avenue for a better economic and a freer intellectual life.

In Sofia the dictionary peddlers sell out fast.

The Central Department Store is called ZUM for short. There the people go shopping to see what's available, not with a list to find what they need. Several stained pink baby buggies are in stock, along with poor-quality nondescript polyester clothing. Rows of empty shelves fill the store; some whole sections are without merchandise. One sign reads: Today We Have Televisions Sold Out. Behind the sign are rows of electrical outlets and antenna sockets.

The ZUM video arcade is jammed with kids playing American games like Astro Blaster and Batman. The instructions are in German. The machines take leva. Fifty stotinki (half a lev) buys a game. That's about eight cents U.S.

It's noon in Lenin Square. A long line of older people wait behind a truck. The truck is from the Swan Restaurant, offering meals to the elderly every Monday in the Square. The hungry look haunted, wrapped up against the cold, clutching empty glass jars and plastic containers for the soup that's ladled out to them in turn. Many make their way over to a few tables set up in the shadow of the Holy Sunday Cathedral. There, some chat as they eat in a leisurely way, trying to make a picnic of their unfortunate situation. Others hunker down over their soup and drink it quickly.

Their plight draws a watching crowd. An Orthodox priest in his black robe with a long, graying beard feeds old bread to the pigeons. Gypsies dance around the soup truck, cackling at the old folks.

"It might get better, but it might get worse," says a middle-aged man who looks around cautiously, worried somebody is watching him talking to foreigners. He's a linguist and insists that the languages he studies not be named. He worries he could be identified by a secret police he still fears.

"There is much more freedom than before. If it were two years before, I could not talk with you here. There would be many secret police. There would be trouble later." But he's still concerned. "I am attentive, I pay attention."

We walk over to the Moscow Café for a coffee. But there is no coffee available. The power is off. There are no hot drinks. We order some sort of milkshakelike affair.

"This is not Poland," he says, looking around to see who is in the café. "This is not Hungary or Czechoslovakia. The old thinking is still here. In Poland people can buy revolvers, just try to buy a revolver here."

Suddenly, the refrigerator compressor kicks on with a rumble, and the coffee shows up. The linguist talks about his recent first trip to Germany. There he encountered Germans who wanted to tell him about the positive aspects of Bulgarian society.

"People told me there is no unemployment in Bulgaria. We do have some, and we will have more. 'You have free medical,' they told me. So does Germany. 'You have free university,' they said. So do Germans, and what kind of job can you have completing Bulgarian university?"

He mused about the pride Bulgarians feel about being patient. "But historically they run out of patience," he worried. "I think it will get worse. I don't know another country where the electric power is stopped."

The troubling thoughts repeated themselves as he considered the future and how Bulgarians will resolve their crisis:

"This is not Poland, this is not Hungary, not Czechoslovakia . . . If something changes, the other things stay . . . In Poland people can buy revolvers. Just try to buy a revolver here."

As we parted, he urged again that his identity be hidden, "They can find me . . ." and he disappeared into Lenin Square.

Bulgarians in line in the cold for basic staples wait huddled with a cup of coffee and a newspaper. They're reading about the rest of the Eastern bloc. They know how tough their life is, especially compared with most of the rest of Europe. "It is the Communist way to take everything," the linguist had said. "Then they give back a tiny piece and say, 'I am giving you something.'" A year after the Berlin Wall opened, Bulgarians are finally ready to force their rulers to give back more than a tiny piece.

Within a couple of weeks, workers joined the striking students. After four days of general strikes throughout the country, the government accepted defeat and resigned. Crowds danced through the streets of Sofia. The parliament struggled to put together a caretaker government to get the country through the winter and promised new elections for the spring. The renamed Communists face a much tougher opposition in those elections. The voters are unlikely to follow a winter of suffering by giving the Communists a third chance at ruling and looting.

Todor Zhivkov watched Bulgaria's second revolution under house arrest, waiting to be tried for corruption during his many years as leader of Bulgaria. He insists he made mistakes but is not a criminal. But he harbors no delusions about the end of his party and its power, laughing when an interviewer brought up Erich Honecker's suggestion that Eastern European Communism will make a comeback. "This," dismissed Zhivkov, "is utter nonsense."

★   ★   ★

Marian sits, watching as Markos and I discuss the lunch menu.

We've been traveling together throughout the East bloc, through revolutions and elections, from bars to embassies. We've become good friends. We speak fast, back and forth, considering what we want to eat and quickly agree on an order for the waiter. Marian smiles, and our lunch choice becomes a symbol to him for the difference between our cultures.

"The mentality of Bulgarians is different," he tells us. "A Bulgarian does not talk without thinking first, the way an American does." He's fascinated by the speed of our menu selections, by the fast and open discussion we had with each other about what to eat. Bulgarians, he tells us, would never interact in such a manner, even good friends, even over something as relatively mundane as what's for lunch. A Bulgarian, says Marian, "stops, thinks, and then says one thing while thinking something else."

Then Marian starts to talk about himself, revealing more differences between Bulgarians and Americans. "My grandfather is a real Yugoslavian gypsy. I told you, but I don't like to say that there is gypsy blood in me. If I say to a company, 'I am a gypsy,' they will say, 'Oh God, he is a gypsy,' because the gypsies here are all thieves. But my friends say it is good to have gypsy blood because it is artistic."

From our American perspective, it isn't much of a revelation. But then our revolutionary actor, our gypsy who is busy overthrowing the government, reminds us of how far Eastern Europe still must travel, what severe problems the region faces.

"I am not a nationalist," says Marian soberly. We are not prepared for what comes next. "But deep in my heart," says Marian without even a trace of a smile, "I hate Turks."

At first I think he's joking, but he's not. "The Turks are a lazy people, Asian." He's not only not joking, he's just warming up.

"They say we are dumb and ugly." He's trying to explain why he hates Turks, and he starts by blaming them. "They say five hundred years we broke you down, and we will break you down again."

He doesn't seem to see the hypocrisy of his revolutionary dreams for a better Bulgaria and his blind prejudice.

"It's in me," he shrugs. "My father, my grandfather, my great-grandfather—they think so because we always fight with Turkey." And this is not just a philosophical attitude. "Me, I have beaten Turkey boys. It's not just for fun. It's something deep in them."

The blind hate—targeting victims not because of any personal animosity—is difficult to comprehend.

"If I'm in a quarrel with them, like in a bar, I fight." Marian really wants to make sure we understand that this feels out of his control. "My mother says, 'Don't fight.' But my father says, 'Fight. Fight. Fight.'"

Chapter Ten

FINALLY ALBANIA

"*Even if we have to go without bread, we Albanians do not violate principles. We do not betray Marxism-Leninism.*"
— Enver Hoxha, founder of post–World War II Albania,
quoted on an Albanian propaganda sign

EVEN AFTER THE revolution in Czechoslovakia, getting a visa to visit there was an expensive and time-consuming proposition for several more months. In the Czechoslovakian military mission in West Berlin, I was filling out the complicated forms in triplicate. Across the desk from me was a fellow with a New Zealand passport.

"You're from New Zealand!" I was enthusiastic. "That means you can go to Albania!"

He looked slowly back at me as if I were crazy.

"Why," he dismissed me, "why would I want to go to Albania?"

It was hard for me to understand why anybody would not jump at the chance to get into Albania. The country is so isolated, geographically and physically, that it offers a glimpse into ancient Europe. The culture, even without taking into consideration the strange effects created by a couple of generations of imposed Stalinism, is so different from that in most of the rest of Europe that a visit could only be a fascinating experience.

Just saying yes and no in Albania is something to look forward to. Yes is the word *po*. No is said *jo*. But tradition adds a shake of the head when you say *po*. And saying *jo* requires an additional nod. To get a feeling for just how different a reversal of those basic gestures can make you feel, try saying yes while you shake your head, and no while you nod. It's hard to do. I know; I tried — not very successfully — in Bulgaria, where the nod means no and the shake yes, too. Then imagine how different just those changed signs would make a journey in a foreign country as remote as Albania. That's reason enough to add Albania to an itinerary.

One of the few guidebooks available for Albania was written by Philip Ward after he visited the country in 1982. He separates Albania from the rest of Eastern Europe, referring to its being behind not the Iron Curtain but the Adriatic Curtain.

"Albania is an intrinsically fascinating state which boasts very little crime," writes Ward, "and suffers very little freedom of action outside the strict confines of puritanical morality. A state where at least officially nobody is unemployed and nobody is rich. Where road accidents are virtually unknown because there are so few vehicles, and because nobody may own a private car. Where miles and miles of golden beaches cannot be over-crowded because there are insufficient hotels."[1]

★   ★   ★

Until 1990, Albania prevented American citizens from touring the little country. But I could think of a long list of reasons to visit the place. For starters, Albania was the only Eastern European country lingering in Stalinist isolation. It seemed unlikely it could buck the trend toward reform for long. Its closed borders, its government's rejection of the rest of the world, and its backward economy meant Albania was a chance to see both the results of complete repression and what prewar Europe

[1]For more details about life in little-known Albania, there are three off-the-beaten-path sources to know about. The Albanian Society, 26 Cambridge Road, Ilford, Essex IG3 8LU, England, offers two periodicals, *Albanian Life* and *Albanian News*. The Albanian Shop, 3 Betterton Street, London WC2H 9BP, is a source for books and handicrafts from Albania. In the U.S., Jack Shulman, P.O. Box 912, New York, NY 10008, operates a private, nonprofit clearinghouse for Albania lore and publishes the annual *Albania Report*.

looked like. Not only that, the beaches must be as spectacular as those in Yugoslavia and Greece; it's the same coastline.[2]

Under the rule of Enver Hoxha, Albania spent a remarkable forty years after World War II isolated from the world. That the country is cut off from the rest of Europe by mountains and minimal transportation facilities made Hoxha's work easier. So did the fact that historically Albania has interacted little with the rest of Europe. In 1948, Hoxha rejected neighbor Yugoslavia because Tito went his own way and defied domination by the Soviet Union. Then in 1960, Hoxha himself rejected the Soviets and took Albania out of the Warsaw Pact because he felt Khruschev was too reform-minded. By the 1970s, China had been rejected by Hoxha because he perceived that China, too, was abandoning the correct Communist path with its domestic and foreign changes.

Despite a few summer street demonstrations—after which several thousand Albanians found refuge in Western embassies and eventually were allowed to leave the country—Albania continued to live in self-exile through 1990. The government continued to have a stranglehold on the population, forcing people not to "violate Marxism-Leninism."

* * *

Leka the First watched the beginning of the unraveling in Albania from a sunnier climate than the Balkan winter can offer. Leka is the exiled king of Albania. He lives in South Africa, near Johannesburg, waiting for the unlikely chance that he'll be called home to reign. He's plotting to recover the throne, hoping to take advantage of the growing turmoil in Albania.

"We, Leka the First, king of Albanians," he announced in a proclamation that at least indicates he knows how to use the royal pronoun, "call upon our people within and outside the

---

[2]Further evidence of Albania's lure for the adventurous can be found in the 1991 Albania tour brochure published by Regent Holidays U.K. Ltd., 13 Small Street, Bristol BS1 1DE, England. Regent is one of the few travel agencies that deals with trips to Albania, and its tours are conducted in English. "Please be prepared for erratic plumbing, carpentry and electric fittings" in the hotels, warns the brochure.

national borders, to take advantage of the events that are shaking the countries of Eastern Europe and rise up, acting in unity and cohesion against the tyrannical and atheist regime that has so long misruled our beloved homeland."

★   ★   ★

Leka says he'll accept the will of his subjects if they decide they want nothing to do with a return to monarchy once the Communists are thrown out. But he says he's convinced he will return triumphantly to Tirana. Not that Leka enjoys much experience as king. His father was King Zog, his mother Queen Geraldine, but Leka was only two days old when Mussolini invaded Albania and the royal family escaped to Greece. Zog died in 1961, and Leka was sworn in as the next king by other exiled Albanians while he was living in Spain.

Spain threw him and his entourage out of that country in 1979 because he was plotting to violently overthrow the Hoxha government. Since then South Africa has provided the hopeful king with a safe haven.

Leka is not alone in hoping that the revolutions in Eastern Europe will spur a return to monarchy. King Michael hopes to take over in Romania; Bulgaria is targeted by Simeon the Second; and Crown Prince Alexander has his eye on Yugoslavia. But after doing without kings and queens for at least half a century, few Eastern Europeans suggest a return of royalty as a solution to their political problems.

Meanwhile, Leka the First keeps himself busy guarding against the assassins he's convinced are out to get him and scheming for his glorious return to the land he left as an infant, and cannot remember.

★   ★   ★

By 1990, even long-time supporters of the Communists in Albania started questioning the government. Either they changed their philosophy after watching the Iron Curtain rise in the rest of Eastern Europe, or they decided that the Albanian Communists were about to go out of business and it was time to choose other allegiances. Most prominent was Ismail Kadare, a writer who is well respected throughout Europe. After supporting Hoxha through the years of oppression, Kadare started criticizing Stalinism as practiced in Albania.

"Democracy, culture, justice, and human rights," he said as he moved to exile in Paris, "are the most fundamental values that every nation is entitled to, and everyone must endorse such a system of values. Law and justice must bring the dark, reactionary forces to their knees. These powers must be destroyed if Albanian society and civilization are to embark on the course of progress."

Then, just before the year ended, it looked as if the Communist government was ending its stranglehold on the people. Already, there had been some of the kind of movement that indicates a change in policies. Diplomatic relations had been renewed with several important countries, including the United States. President Ramiz Alia allowed a few domestic changes that he termed "democratization." For the first time since 1967, private religious services were officially permitted. Farmers could privately sell produce and meat, and borders were opened for Albanians who wanted to see the rest of the world. President Alia warmed relations with the West and announced interest in a market economy. But still he, and the Communist Party he leads, remained in tight control.

Visas for journalists were rare, but in early November 1990, David Bender managed a trip for the *New York Times*. He reported from Kavajë on the anti-Communist demonstrations:

> The current confusion in the Government handling of the security situation was illustrated when several foreign correspondents visited Kavajë on a recent afternoon. Admitted originally with visas seemingly permitting more or less free movement in Albania for ten or more days, they were abruptly told that they could only visit Durrës and that it would be desirable if they departed the country as soon as convenient. They stopped in Durrës and then proceeded toward Tirana by way of Kavajë, ten miles to the south.
>
> A few minutes after they turned up in Kavajë, four cars carrying uniformed and plainclothes policemen suddenly appeared. The journalists were escorted northward toward a jail for inter-

rogation. All at once an official from another Government department appeared and persuaded the police to let the correspondents go with a warning not to repeat such deviations from the prescribed route.

By 1990 tourist visits were finally allowed for Americans. I found a travel agency in Germany that specialized in tours to Albania and arranged for a tourist visa for me and Markos, traveling under the guise of elementary schoolteachers. Then we waited to see if the government was going to fall before the end of the year.

It was touch and go around Christmastime; rioting hit again in the middle of December in Tirana, Shkodër, and Kavajë. The familiar chants came from the demonstrations: "Reforms!" "No dictatorship!" "Democracy!" "Don't lie!" The familiar explanations came from the official news agency: Demonstrators "committed acts of vandalism." They were opposed by "citizens of Shkodër, workers, Communists." Rioting was stopped by "forces of public order and the army." President Ramiz Alia showed up on national television calling for calm.

Then Alia quickly started changing the rules of the game and bought himself and his government some time. He reversed a Communist Party order that had stood since 1946 and that permitted no opposition political parties in Albania. Immediately, at a huge rally in Tirana establishment of the Democratic Party was announced, led by a university economics professor, Gramoz Pashko. The crowd yelled "Democracy! Democracy!" But the government held on. Pashko expressed his appreciation to Alia for introducing the multiparty system and started campaigning for the election scheduled a few months later. Alia kept maneuvering, admitting "mistakes were made," explaining that a new Communist Party platform would "deviate from many of the principles of socialism" and "correct many of the attitudes of the past," but that it did "not intend to abandon its Marxist ideology."

The year ended, and the Communist Party held on to power. I must say, I felt a certain amount of relief. It would have been hard to stay away from Albania if the Communist government fell there too, but since it didn't, I decided not to go. By the end of 1990, I had realized that I'd had my fill of standing out in the freezing Eastern European cold with thousands of miserable and abused people overthrowing their government. I was tired of ordering a salad and then working my way through another plate of pickles. I'd had enough of overcast skies and brown coal smoke.

It's not that I wish the Albanians any more oppression. Certainly they've had their share. They've been kept from the twentieth century, left farming by hand and working in antiquated industrial squalor. Students live in slum dormitories, political opponents languish in prison.

If the lessons of 1989 and 1990 in Eastern Europe are the guide that they should be, then Albanians, either with the election, or sooner in the streets, will shed their dictators and take their own road to renewal. Or, possibly, the Communist Party will be able to realign its operation fast enough and radically enough to hold on to power and orchestrate the recovery while staying in control. That scenario seems highly unlikely though, given the grief the Party has caused so many Albanians for so many years.

But, one way or another, President Alia and his government are already making it clear that the bad old days are passing. Just in time for a Christmas present, the statue of Stalin in Tirana was loaded onto a truck and hauled out of sight.

Epilogue

MEANWHILE, BACK
IN THE NEW WORLD

*"I am convinced we will look back on November 1989 as a dark day
in history. These Germans started two world wars this century, and
they will start another. They want to dominate the world. I worry
that my sons will fight still another war against the united
Germany."*

— Upset member of a California Rotary Club
during a lunchtime discussion about the new Germany,
Summer 1990

AFTER A LONG flight back to America from Berlin, spending the
night near the airport seemed like the best idea. Immediately
the negative stereotypes of America started collapsing.

A taxi driver directed a puzzled and lost stranger to a cheaper
bus, instead of hustling him into the cab.

The bus driver made a point of showing a couple of other
foreigners the difference between an American one- and ten-
dollar bill, so they wouldn't get gypped. "Careful with those
tens!" he called again to them as they headed off after the
lesson.

And this was New York.

Other stereotypes were reinforced.

As the shuttle bus made its way from the old Icelandair DC-8
to the terminal building, a crummy speaker blasted, "Good
golly, Miss Molly . . ." The volume was so loud, it was difficult
to talk. How crass and uncultured. How American! It is impossible to imagine a German airport bus filled with blaring pop

music. At first it struck me as funny, the rock and roll, with too much bass and so loud the sound was distorted, cranking through the bus speakers. Then I was momentarily annoyed, before realizing that the raw reality of the intrusion into my privacy was somehow comforting.

"Wake up from your jet lag. Dance. Accept what the driver wants to hear; he's the guy stuck pushing a bus back and forth across the airport all day." That was the message that quickly replaced my irritation. By the time we got to the terminal, I was tapping my foot. "Good golly, Miss Molly!" — it's a great American tune.

The hotel was early sixties, too. It was directly in front of the freeway, and whatever luster it might have had once upon a time was long gone. The airline had recommended it as cheap, clean, and safe.

The hundred dollars a night included cigarette burns on the bedspreads, a lumpy bed and well-worn rug, scratched and dented triple locks on the doors, a funky bathroom, and a color TV.

The lead local news story on the TV screamed: "Two kids found dead. Police see no connection between the murders and the coconuts and dead chickens found near the bodies." Really.

In the basement, the hotel restaurant was called the Khasbah Supper Club. The lights were dim and reflected from the mirrored ball slowly spinning over the bar, the same type of contraption that swirled in the Prague hotel where the barmaid had told me she was forced to risk her life for the sake of her daughter.

In the Khasbah, those lights played against the pasty face of the loud bleached blonde holding court with a couple of friends and the bartender.

"He's living with some bimbo in Staten Island," she complained. Her country's revolution was over two hundred years old. She had her freedom, and her memories.

"When you go out with him, there's no one better. He's got charisma, chutzpa, balls — you name it."

"Can I take the chips?" I asked when there was a lull.

"You take 'em, honey. We don't want 'em. They're stale."

I was home.

Home in America after watching the Iron Curtain rise. Back with an appreciation for what the last couple of generations of oppression did to the Old World, appreciation for the shock caused by sudden liberation. I was returning with a new sense of what it means to be an American.

One day as my friend Dagmar was talking about the business side of her work as an artist, I suggested it was probably time that she equipped herself with business cards. "Oh, no," was her response, "I couldn't, not until I am a well-established artist." I tried to explain to Dagmar how many of us in America made sure we walked around armed with documents like business cards just as soon as we came up with an idea for something we may want to do. I told her a business card, a sign on the door, or a listing in the telephone book put us in a position to get a new enterprise going. It was an alien concept for her. In her European mind, first you proved yourself, validated your existence; then you could consider reaping the rewards. It is the self-confident arrogance of America that allows us to conceptualize ideas and then feel we can easily live out the fantasies we generate. It may be presumptuous, but in America we've often prospered just because we've been too sure of ourselves to doubt that we could become whoever we said we were on our freshly printed business cards.

And I was back in America contemplating one of the questions I was asked so often while commuting back and forth across the Atlantic: Are the Germans still dangerous?

It was a question that was made much more difficult to answer by the American response to Saddam Hussein's invasion of Kuwait. It's so simple to keep blaming the Germans as a group for the crimes of Hitler. Easy, but wrong, as Václav Havel made clear in his speech comparing anti-German behavior to anti-Semitism. Once the last German born before 1945 dies, there will be no further rationalization for even considering a sweeping indictment of Germans as a dangerous nationality.

Rather than watching out for a resurgence of German evil, surely World War II and the cold war have taught us that our energies are better spent fighting human evil whatever its nationality. With Saddam Hussein brutally invading Kuwait, and with America leading the bloody charge to remove him, there's little room for singling out Germans as militaristic. Even though German companies did sell Hussein his bunkers and death gases, so did hundreds of thousands of individual Germans take to the streets protesting the decision to counter Hussein with force before trying a lasting trade embargo. One man, a German writer named Walter Jens, even opened his home to American soldiers stationed in Germany who were avoiding service in the Gulf; he said two GIs took him up on his offer to hide them from the American authorities.

★　★　★

It was at little Westminster College in Fulton, Missouri, that then former prime minister Winston Churchill made his Iron Curtain speech. "A shadow has fallen upon the scenes so lately lighted by the Allied victory," Churchill told his audience. "Nobody knows what Soviet Russia and its Communist international organization intends to do in the immediate future, or what are the limits, if any, to their expansive and proselytizing tendencies. I have strong admiration and regard for the valiant Russian people and my wartime comrade, Marshal Stalin," said Churchill. Then, that March 5, 1946, he lit into his bleak and accurate forecast.

> It is my duty, however, for I am sure you would wish me to state the facts as I see them to you, to place before you certain facts about the present position in Europe.
> From Stettin in the Baltic to Trieste in the Adriatic, an iron curtain has descended across the Continent. Behind that line lie all the capitals of the ancient states of central and eastern Europe. Warsaw, Berlin, Prague, Vienna, Budapest, Belgrade, Bucharest, and Sofia, all these famous cities and the populations around them lie in what I must call the Soviet sphere, and all are subject in one form or another, not only to Soviet influence, but to a very high and, in many cases, increasing measure of control from Moscow. Athens alone — Greece with its immortal glories — is free to decide its future at an election under British, American,

and French supervision. The Russian-dominated Polish government has been encouraged to make enormous and wrongful inroads upon Germany, and mass expulsions of millions of Germans on a scale grievous and undreamed of are now taking place. The Communist parties, which were very small in all these eastern states of Europe, have been raised to pre-eminence and power far beyond their numbers and are seeking everywhere to obtain totalitarian control.

Churchill's analysis was correct, and he knew it. "I have felt bound to portray the shadow which, alike in the west and in the east, falls upon the world." Then he proceeded to offer a solution for stopping Moscow's expansion: "From what I have seen of our Russian friends and Allies during the war, I am convinced that there is nothing they admire so much as strength, and there is nothing for which they have less respect than for weakness, especially military weakness. For that reason the old doctrine of a balance of power is unsound. We cannot afford, if we can help it, to work on narrow margins, offering temptations to a trial of strength."

For the next forty-three years, East and West squared off against each other along that Iron Curtain, ready to fight to the finish. But by July 6, 1989, McDonald's was setting up shop in Moscow, and Gorbachev, not Stalin, was running the Soviet Union. At Strasbourg that day, Gorbachev made his "Common European Home" speech, and reversed the scenario painted by Churchill: "Now that the twentieth century is drawing to a close and the postwar period and the cold war are becoming things of the past," Gorbachev told the Council of Europe, "the Europeans are beginning to face the unique opportunity of playing their role in building a new world, a role that is worthy of their history and their economic and intellectual potential."

This speech came shortly after the Tiananmen Square massacre in China; Gorbachev had seen the beginning of this conflict during his visit to Beijing. As he spoke, Gorbachev made it clear that the Brezhnev Doctrine — the Soviet policy of forcing its colonies to stay within the Soviet sphere — was over: "European states belong to different social systems. That is a reality.

Recognition of this historical fact and respect for the sovereign right of every nation freely to choose a social system constitute the major prerequisites for a normal European process."

In case some listeners were not certain about his message, he added these details: "Social and political orders in one or another country have changed in the past and may change in the future. But this change is the exclusive affair of the people of that country and is their choice." And just to make sure nobody missed the new policy statement, Gorbachev spelled out the new rules from Moscow: "Any interference in domestic affairs and any attempts to restrict the sovereignty of states—friends, allies, or any others—are inadmissible."

Then Gorbachev offered his vision for cooperation instead of confrontation:

> There are and can be no "strangers" in efforts to build European peace—all are equal partners here, and every country, including neutral and nonaligned countries, bears its share of responsibility to its people and to Europe. The philosophy of the "common European home" concept rules out the probability of an armed clash and the very possibility of the use of force or the threat of force—alliance against alliance, inside the alliance, wherever. This philosophy suggests that a doctrine of restraint should take the place of the doctrine of deterrence. This is not just a play on words, but the logic of European development prompted by life itself.

So he said it once, he said it twice, and he said it yet again that day. Every nation has a right to freely choose its social system, no interference in the domestic affairs of sovereign states, no threat or use of force inside the alliances. By November, just a few months later, the Berlin Wall was history.

★　★　★

Only the Albanians stayed home when the cold war officially ended late in November 1990. All the other European leaders joined with the Americans and the Canadians to celebrate peace and happiness in Paris. The host, French president François Mitterrand, told the meeting and the world, "It is the

first time in history that we witness a change in the depth of the
European landscape which is not the outcome of a war or bloody
revolution. We do not have sitting here either victors or vanquished, but free countries equal in dignity. For more than
forty years," Mitterrand reminded everyone, "we have known
stability without freedom. Henceforth, we want freedom in
stability."[1]

But, ominously, Mitterrand shared the headlines the next day
with news from Baghdad that Iraq was sending more occupying
troops to Kuwait.

★　★　★

The euphoria that wafted around the globe as the Iron Curtain
rose was pitifully short-lived. The end of the cold war removed
the fear of imminent nuclear destruction and added the hope of
a peace dividend, money that could be spent on social progress
instead of weapons. While the world was still thrilled by such
positive ideas, the Persian Gulf war made it clear that there
would be no peace yet, and certainly no peace dividend.

At the same time, Eastern Europe became aware that the road
to a successful market economy was going to be a long and
difficult one. For most, the luxuries of the West were still
unavailable. The emerging democracies were already getting
much less help than they expected, needed, and wanted from
the West. The ethnic, nationalist, and linguistic conflicts that
were returning to the region worsened.

In 1989 and 1990 Eastern Europe was the darling of the West,
filled with brave revolutionaries who threw off their oppressors.
The revolutions and elections were proof to the West that
Communism was a failure, capitalism the correct path; they
were vindication for the postwar policies of the West. But by
1991, the West was satiated with Eastern Europe. It was as if the
attention span of the West was too short for people and institutions to stay involved and interested during the long recovery

---

[1]The occasion was a meeting of the thirty-four-member Conference on
Security and Cooperation in Europe where an arms reduction treaty was
signed, aggression was rejected, and both free elections and free market
economies were endorsed.

period that Eastern Europe must work through. Communism was defeated; that was cause for celebration. But the ongoing problems of the region were so much less dramatic and exciting that the West lost interest.

With Hungary filling up with homeless people, unemployment soaring in Poland, prices surging in Czechoslovakia, Yugoslavia falling apart, the low standard of living unchanged in eastern Germany, with Communists still governing in Bulgaria and Romania, Eastern Europe could well surprise the West. The Eastern bloc will regain the headlines fast if the Communists make a comeback by offering once more the promises they kept for over forty years: order in the streets and adequate — if marginal — food and shelter.

Some pessimistic observers (and participants) of the postrevolutionary period came up with this depressing description of the mood: "Eastern Europeans are finding the tunnel at the end of the light."

The West should pay more attention, if for no other than selfish reasons. As problems persist in Eastern Europe, the West could find itself seriously considering an installation of its own version of the Iron Curtain to protect its interests from swarms of hundreds of thousands, even millions, of refugees coming West to escape poverty and violence. Just like the yuppie medical student I encountered before the Wall came down who feared competition from East German doctors, much of Western Europe is getting nervous. The line that used to mark the Iron Curtain could soon resemble the Mexican border with the United States, blocked by a Western European border patrol trying to turn back a surge of wretched migrants.

Already, at the end of 1990, Austria was patrolling its border with Hungary, looking for desperate Romanians and Bulgarians heading West across Hungary. Just like the American patrols working the Mexican border, a few thousand Austrian soldiers were busy in jeeps and helicopters using searchlights and special night-vision glasses to look for unwanted immigrants and turning them back to the miserable lives they hoped to leave behind.

★ ★ ★

Some German friends came to visit us in California after the
Wall fell. It was a typically beautiful sunny day, and we spent it
picnicking along a creek in the countryside. They had been
traveling much of the summer across America. But one of them
was particularly troubled by what he had been reading in the
newspapers. His command of English was excellent, but he still
missed a word here and there.

"Why," he asked, "are the American authorities poisoning all
the gypsies?"

We tried to convinced him that no such thing was occurring,
but he was adamant. "I read about it in the newspaper!"

Finally we figured out that he had just skipped over a word he
didn't know, the key word *moths*.

We laughed, but the misunderstanding left me troubled. He
actually believed—this German tourist as he wandered around
America—that the U.S. government was systematically killing
gypsies.

NOTE ON DIACRITICS AND PLACE NAMES

The languages used in Eastern Europe make use of a wide variety of diacritical marks. Some, such as the umlaut in German, are familiar to those who read the English language and they have been incorporated into American English. Häagen Dazs ice cream simply invented its name to sound foreign; it comes from New Jersey. Other marks, for example the slashed el in Polish, are rarely, if ever, seen in English. In this book, only those diacritical marks in relatively common English usage are retained in the text.

The native names of nations rarely correspond to the label they have been given in English. For clarity, the Eastern European nations are usually referred to in the text by their English names. But an awareness of the appellations people use themselves for their countries adds texture to any study of foreign cultures, even when the names are unfamiliar. So on the maps of the region in this book, the names used locally are not translated.

SELECT BIBLIOGRAPHY

This partial bibliography lists a variety of options for further reading about the region.

Eastern Europe on a Shoestring was published in 1989, before the Wall came down, by Lonely Planet. Written by David Stanley, it offers a pretty comprehensive compilation of where to go and how to get there. Especially in retrospect, some of Stanley's naive attitudes toward the old dictatorships are, at best, amusing. "You'll find no iron curtain here," he writes in his introduction — putting iron curtain in quotes — and goes on to insist, "unless you come looking for one."

Also published just before the Wall came down was *Wall: The Inside Story of Divided Berlin* by Peter Wyden (Simon and Schuster, 1989). The book offers fascinating detail about the construction of the Wall in 1961.

The Rise and Fall of the Third Reich by William Shirer (Simon and Schuster, 1959) provides an accessible grounding in the events that led up to the establishment of the Iron Curtain.

A couple of novels to get into the postwar German mood: *Headbirths, or The Germans Are Dying Out*, Günter Grass (Ballantine, 1984), and *How German Is It*, Walter Abish (New Directions, 1980).

A provocative short-story collection is *Voices East and West, German Short Stories Since 1945*, edited and translated by Roger Norton (Frederick Ungar, 1984).

A collection of Günter Grass's speeches and writings on the German question can be found in *Two States — One Nation?* a volume published in 1990 by Harcourt Brace Jovanovich.

A couple of novels for a glimpse at prerevolutionary Czechoslovakia: Milan Kundera's *The Unbearable Lightness of Being* (Faber and Faber, 1988) and *Utz* by Bruce Chatwin (Penguin, 1988). Kundera is sometimes criticized for shaping Czechoslovakia into his own erotic fantasy from the safety of his Paris exile. For another view, try now-President Václav Havel's *Letters to Olga* (Knopf, 1988), the letters he wrote to his wife from prison.

For a thorough overview of Eastern Europe (except Albania), Flora Lewis's *Europe, A Tapestry of Nations* (Simon and Schuster, 1987), is a good beginning.

For Albania, *Albania, a Travel Guide* by Philip Ward (Oleander Press, 1987) is a helpful start.

An intriguing look at the cultural differences between the New and Old Worlds can be found in *Painted in Blood, Understanding Europeans* by Stuart Miller (Atheneum, 1987).

Another valuable introduction to the Continental mentality, and its interaction with America, comes from Luigi Barzini in his *The Europeans* (Penguin, 1985).

To keep in touch with ongoing developments in Eastern Europe from a local perspective, the handful of indigenous English-language newspapers are fascinating:

The Warsaw Voice
ul. Bagatela 12, 00–585 Warszawa, Poland

Daily News of the Hungarian News Agency
P.O. Box 3, H–1425, Budapest, Hungary

Sofia News
113 Lenin Blvd., 1184 Sofia, Bulgaria

Politika, the International Weekly
29 Makedonska, Belgrade, Yugoslavia

Prognosis
Dlouda trida 12, 110 00 Praha 1, Czechoslovakia

The *Eastern European Reporter* is an independent English-language quarterly publishing essays, articles, and documents written by Eastern Europeans about the changes in their region. It is available at 71 Belmont Avenue, London N17 6AX.

ACKNOWLEDGMENTS

My experiences behind the Iron Curtain were made full and rich by the openness of the people I encountered there. Many of them are identified by name in these pages; many others were helpful even if their specific stories are not included.

A project like this relies on a thorough support system, and several friends and colleagues offered needed help. Scott French took time away from his own writing to read work in progress. Chris Slattery, Don Chamberlain, and Michael Hassan were valuable sounding boards. Lynne Hughes and Chandler Laughlin provided crucial computer hardware and helped develop my computer literacy.

Special appreciation goes to Gene Gardner for use of his Sausalito office — the lack of windows minimized distraction — and to Sigrid Akkermann, not only for sharing her crowded Berlin apartment with a smile, but also for all her help with research.

My thanks to the American Council on Germany for providing me with a John J. McCloy Fellowship for travel to Germany, and to Helga Dougherty for her German language tutorials. I must also acknowledge the Robert Bosch Foundation for travel and study opportunities in Europe, while chastising them for attempting to control the activities of their fellows. I advise the Bosch Foundation that history clearly teaches us that intellectual freedom, not propaganda, is the path to better international understanding.

News-gathering assignments from ABC and CBS sent me through the Iron Curtain during these exciting times, and for that I am appreciative to those editors and producers who recognized the continuing importance of the Eastern European story, even after the Berlin Wall fell.

I can trace my interest in Eastern Europe to stories told to me by my father, Thomas Laufer, and his memory was with me while I traveled and wrote. Important lessons in gathering information came from my mother, Eva Laufer, and I enjoyed profitable encouragement for this book from my sons, Michael Laufer and Talmage Morris.

My wife, Sheila Swan Laufer, provided invaluable encouragement and assistance throughout the adventure.

Finally, I wish to thank my editors, Thomas Christensen and Anne Dickerson, publisher William Brinton, and all of the staff at Mercury House for their early and continuing enthusiasm for this project.

ABOUT THE AUTHOR

SCOTT FRENCH

PETER LAUFER has many years of experience as a free-lance international reporter for both newspapers and radio. His first overseas assignment — for the legendary San Francisco radio station KSAN — was to track down Timothy Leary in Europe after he'd fled the States. In the intervening two decades, Laufer has worked for several years as an NBC news correspondent from that network's Washington bureau, reported extensively for the ABC radio network, and recently covered the revolutions and elections in Eastern Europe as well as the invasion of Kuwait for the CBS radio stations. The *Washington Post* and the *San Francisco Chronicle*, among other newspapers, have published his reports on such major news stories as the war in Nicaragua, cocaine trafficking in Colombia, and the 1989 San Francisco earthquake. His television experience includes a stint as guest host of "CBS News Nightwatch."

A regular columnist for the *SF Weekly*, Laufer is also an affiliate artist at the Headlands Center for the Arts. His professional honors include the B'nai B'rith Edward R. Murrow and Long Island University George Polk awards, and the 1991 Excellence in Professional Achievement Award from the Society of Professional Journalists. He lives in Marin County, California.

This book was designed by Sharon Smith.
The text is set in Electra, a typeface
designed in 1935 by William Addison Dwiggins.
Neither "old style" nor "modern," this simple, fluid, readable face
charts its own path in typographic style.
The maps were created by Robert Schwarzenbach.
All photographs are by the author.
Typesetting was done at Mercury House by Chet Shaw.
R. R. Donnelley & Sons did the printing and binding.
The editor was Thomas Christenson and
the assistant editor Anne Dickerson.
Production was coordinated by Zipporah Collins and Hazel White.
The copyeditor was Virginia Rich and
the proofreader Alice Klein.